# Keith Pepperell

# Pictures VI

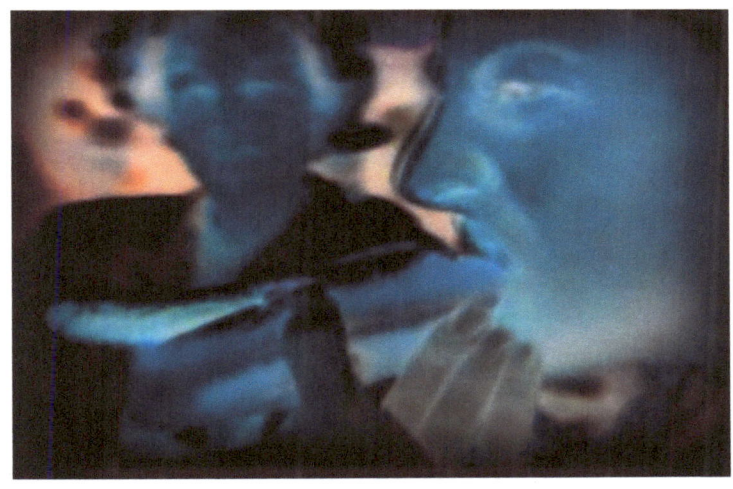

# Keith Pepperell

## DEDICATION

As always to my spawn Jack, Lydia, and Alex all of whom have snapped from time to time

# ACKNOWLEDGMENTS

LADY JOAN PEPPERELL

SIR FRANCIS PEPPERELL

SIR ARTHUR MACDONALD (DON)  FOWLER

LADY AUDREY FOWLER

Keith Pepperell

# IMAGES

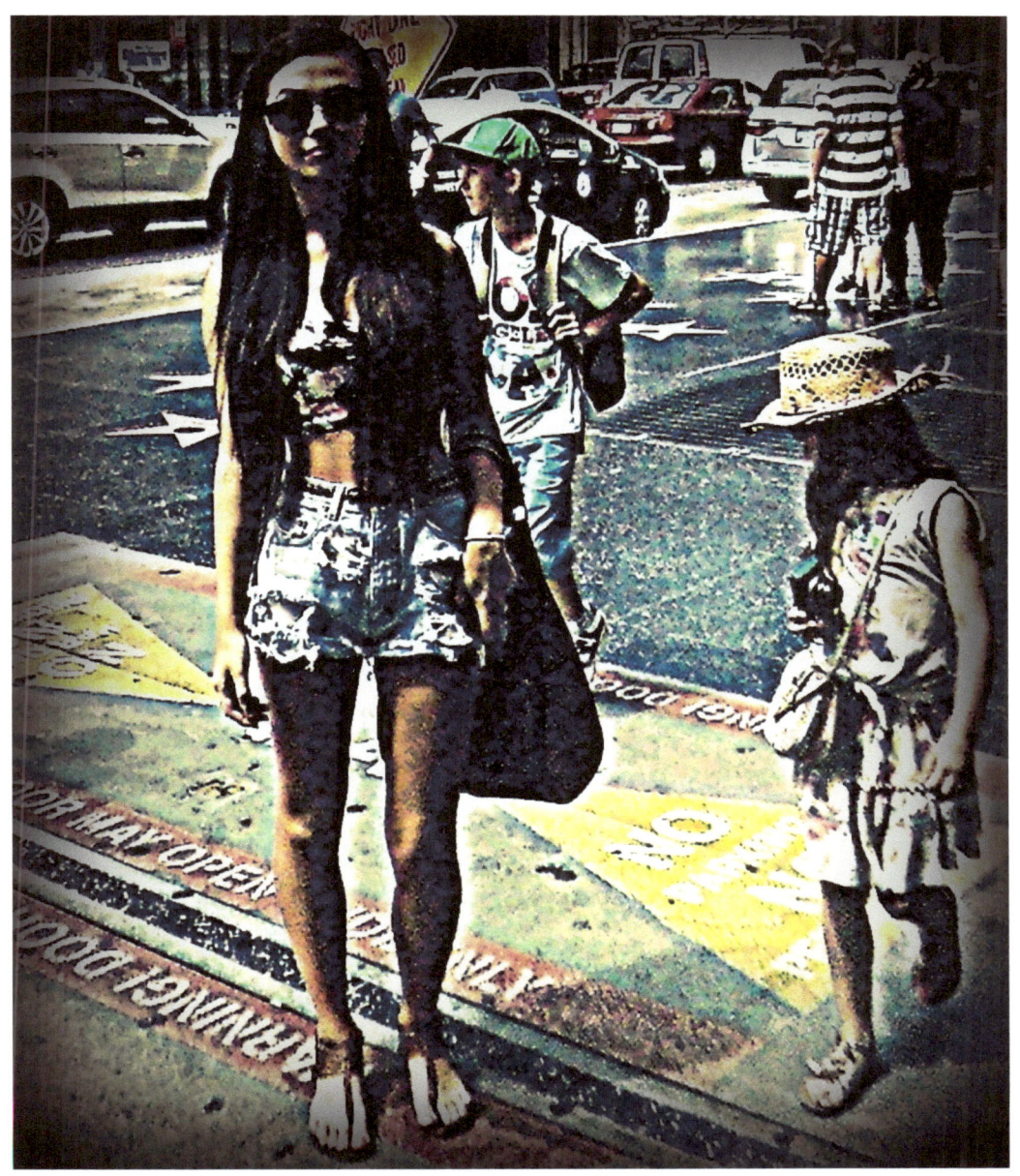

Alex in Hollywood

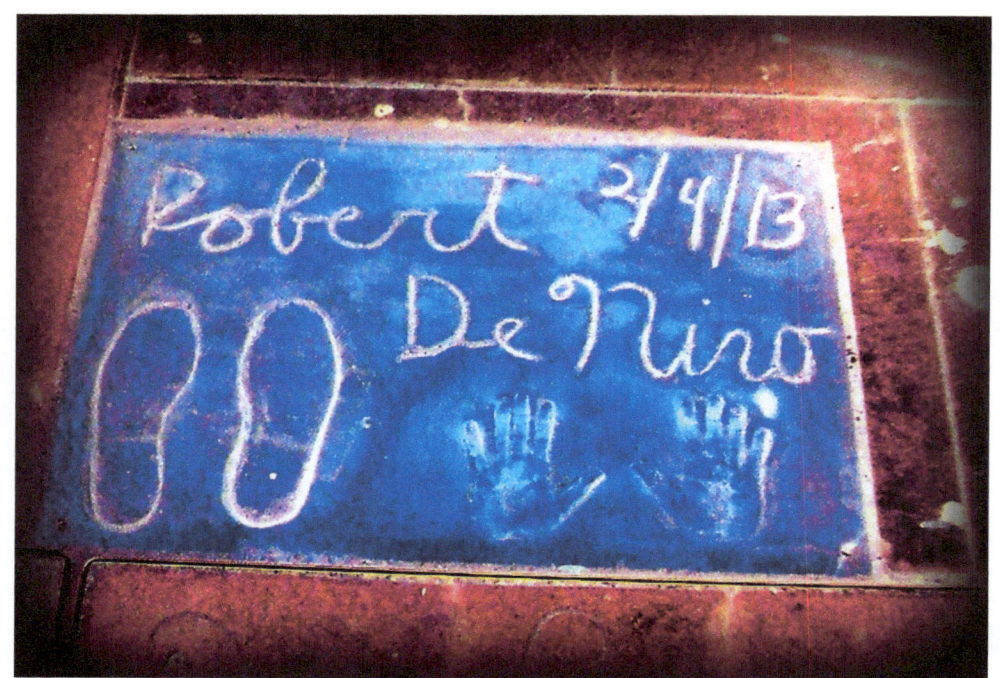

Chinese Theater

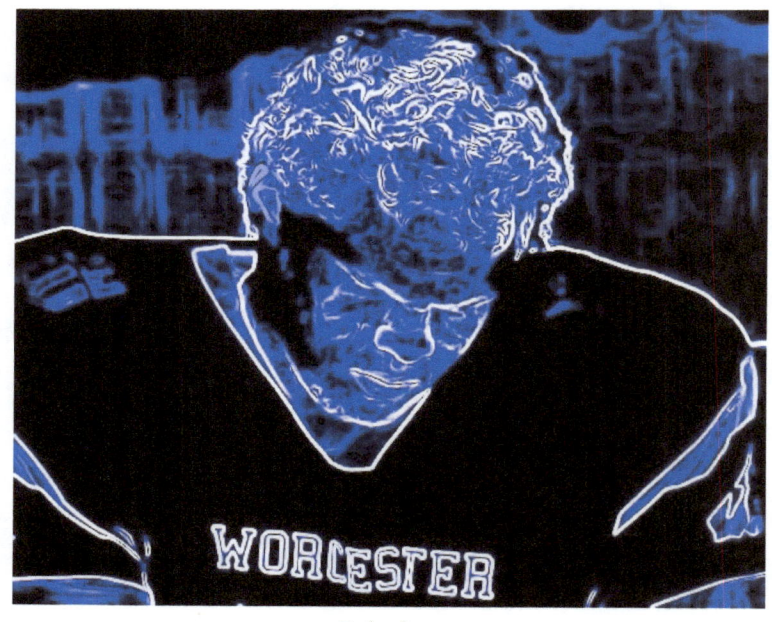

Okko

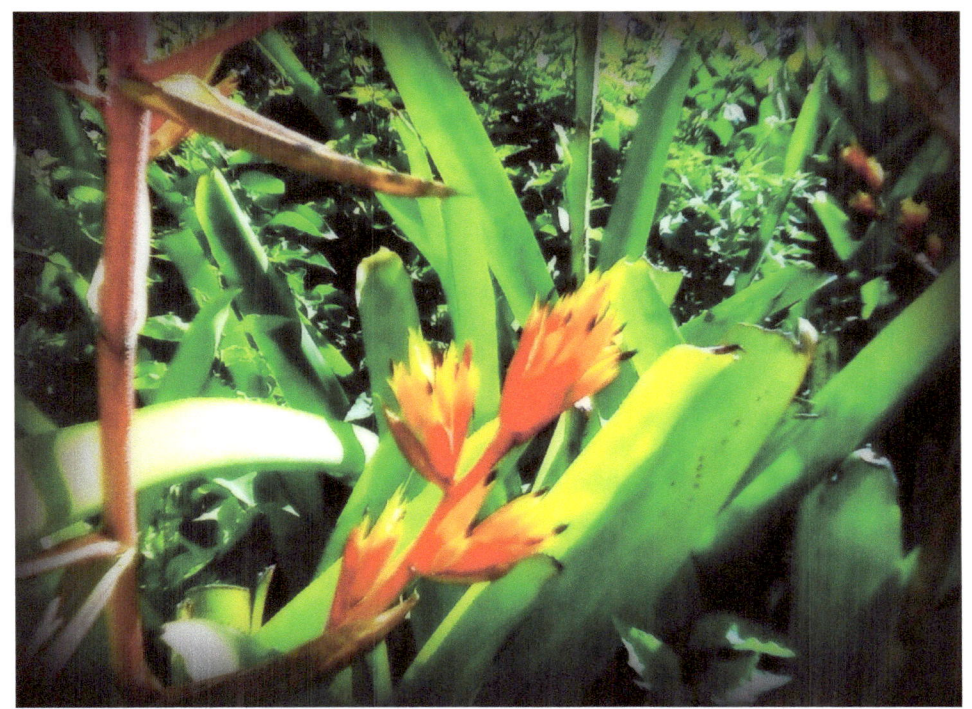

A Little Vegetation

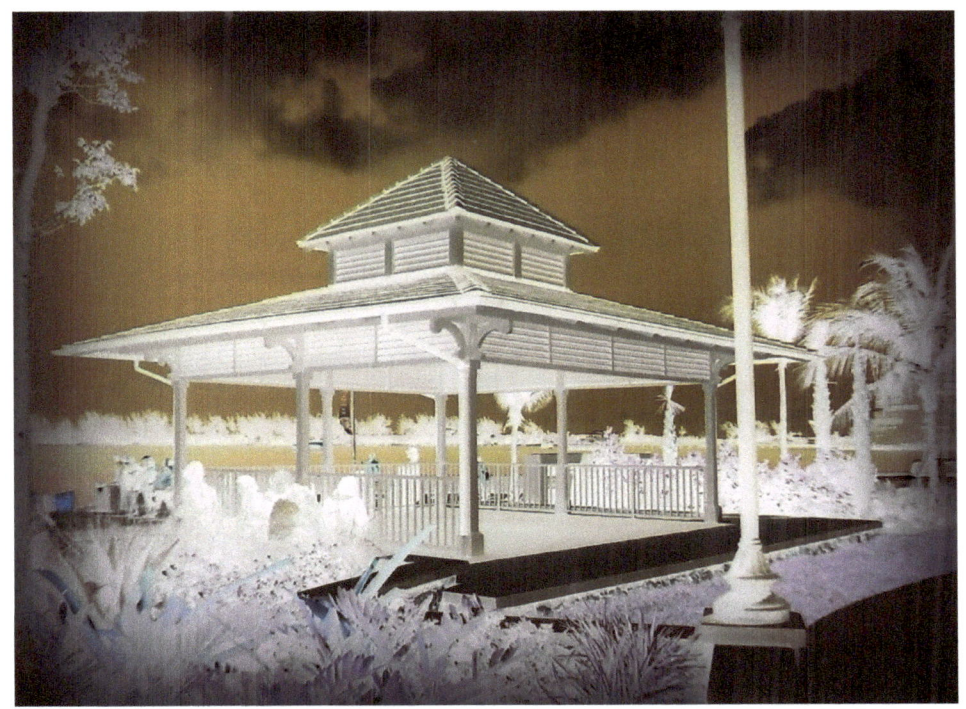

Bandstand

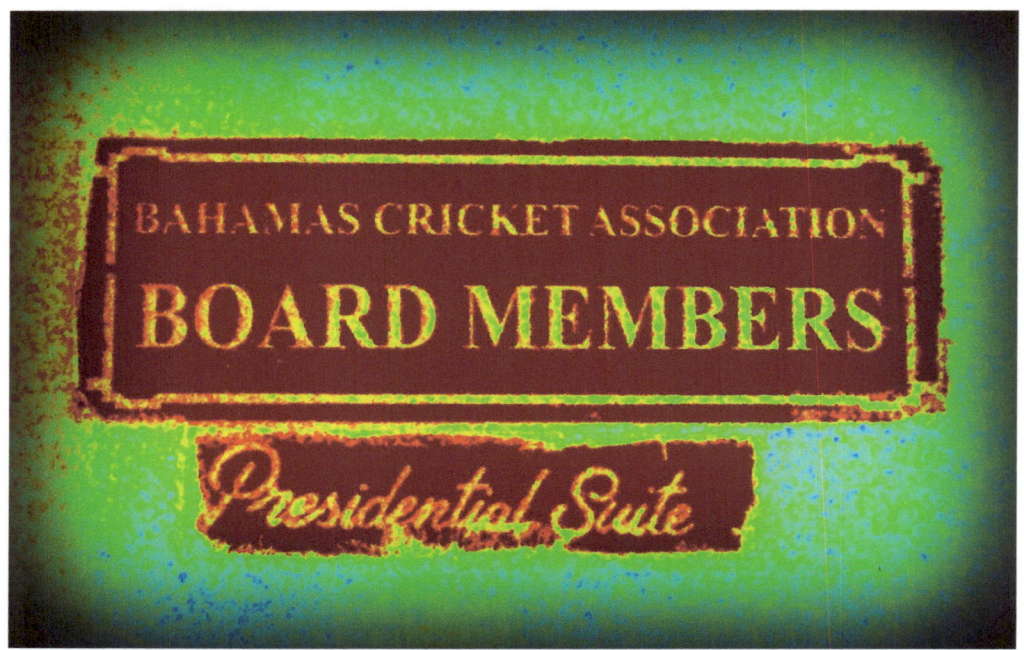

Presidential Suite

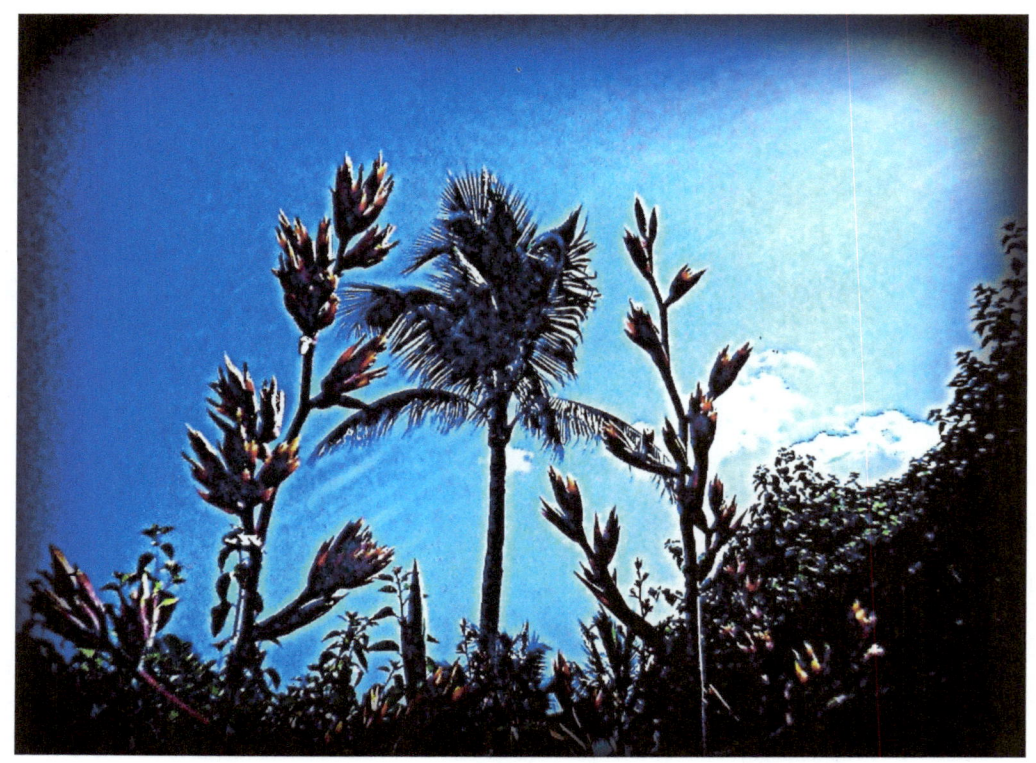

Bahamian Trees

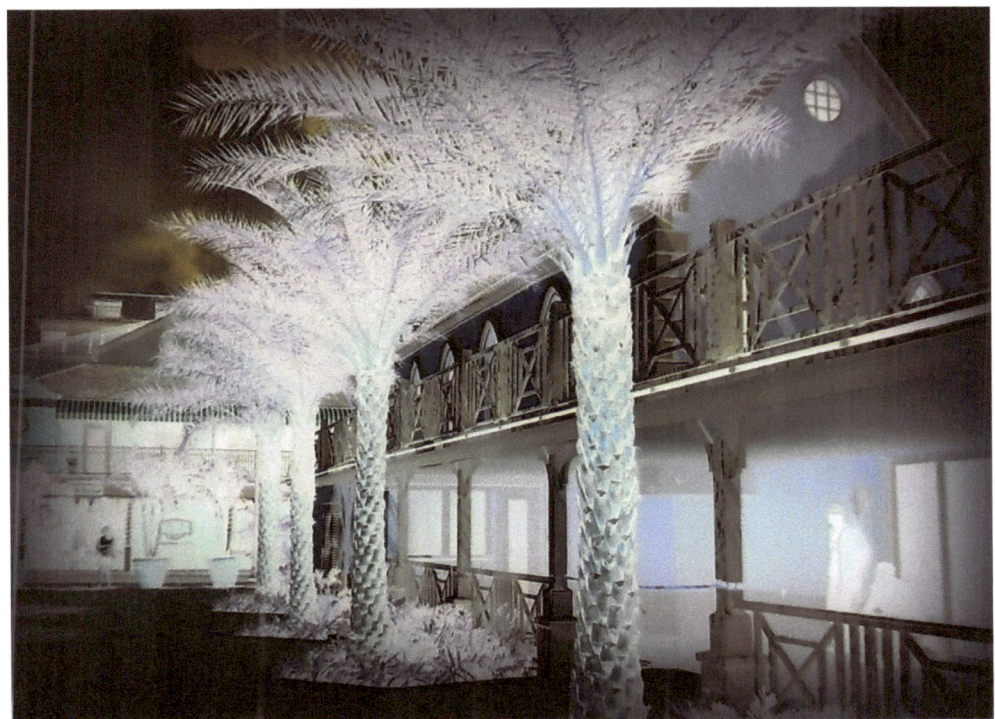

The Courtyard

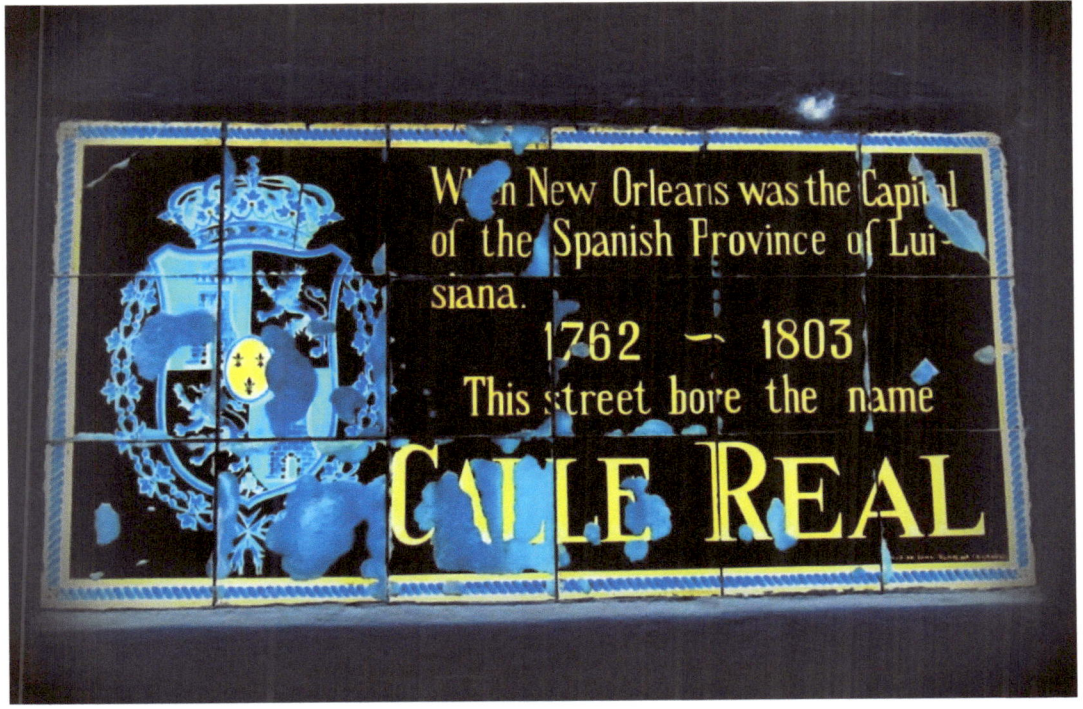

Calle Real

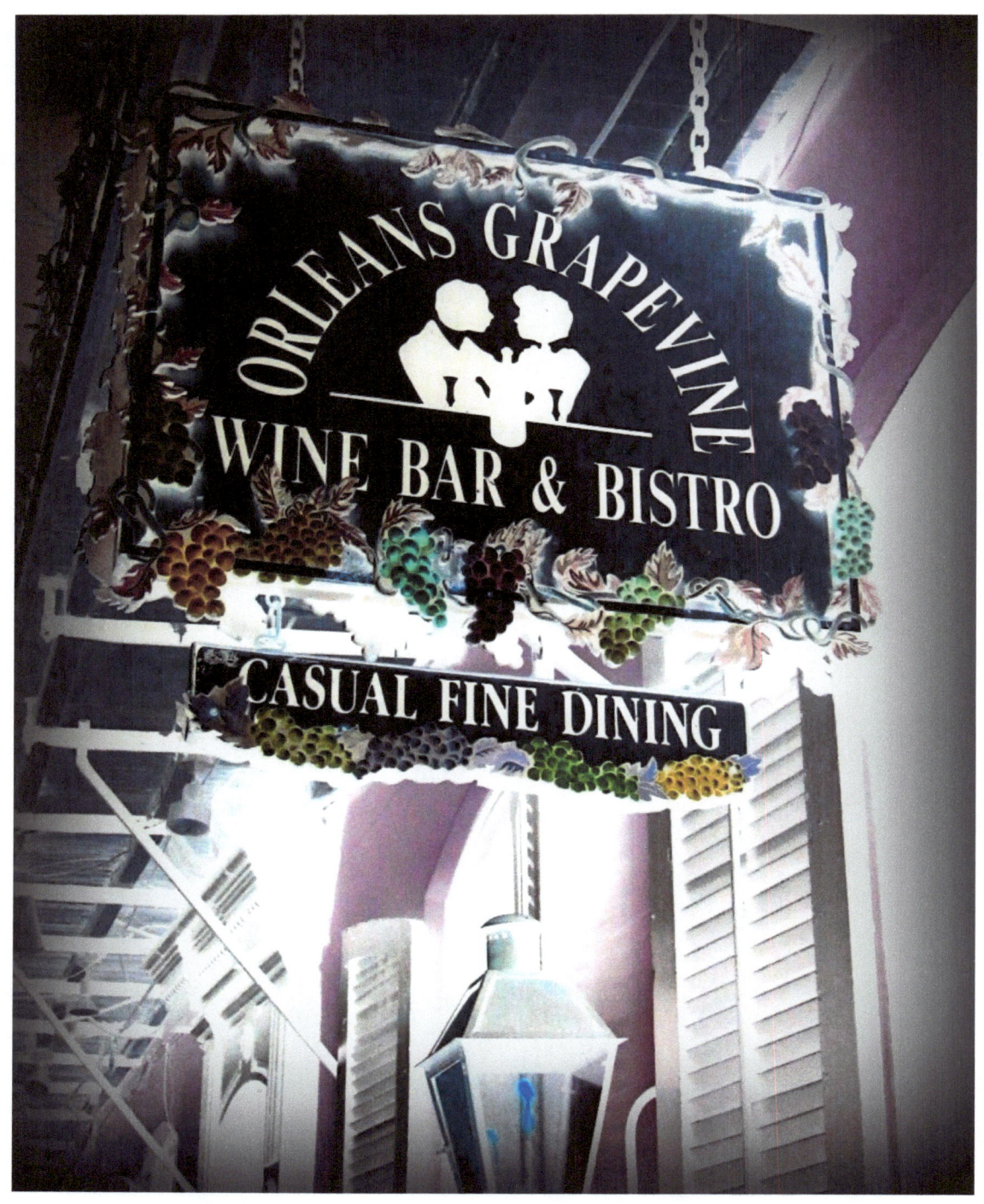

Lunchtime

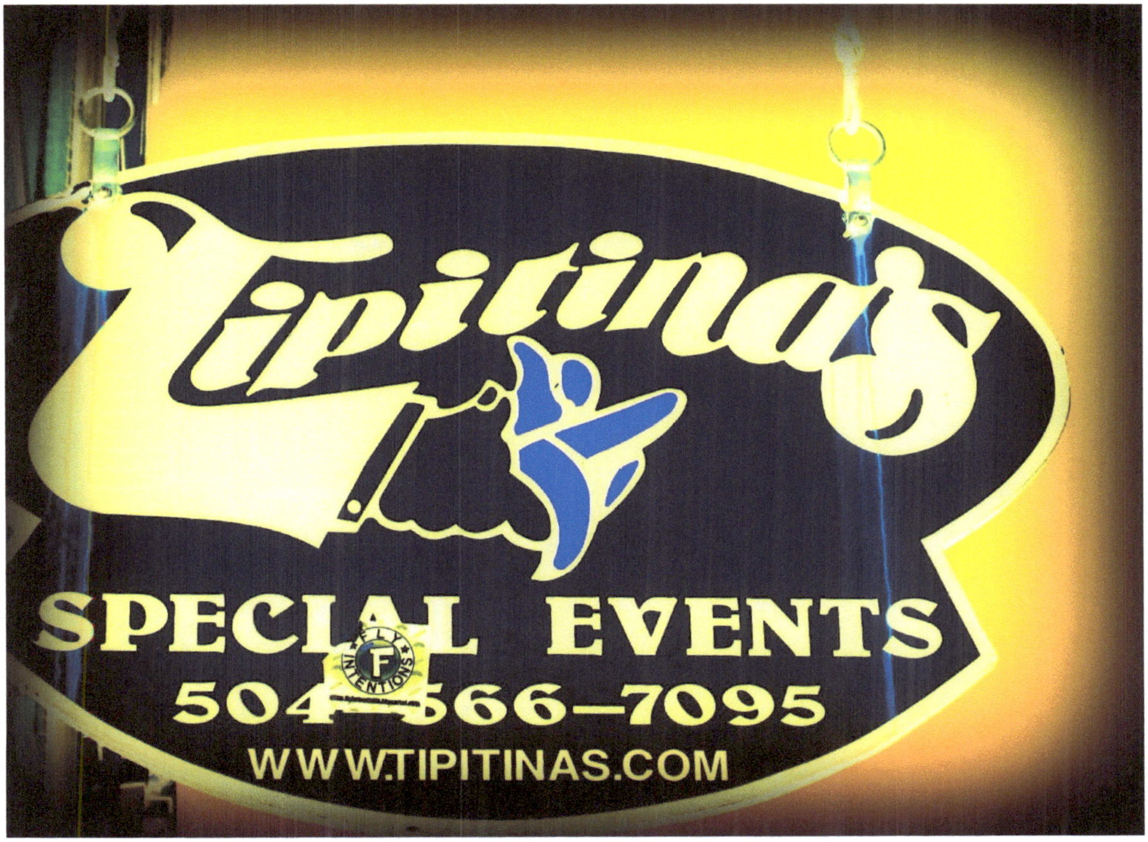

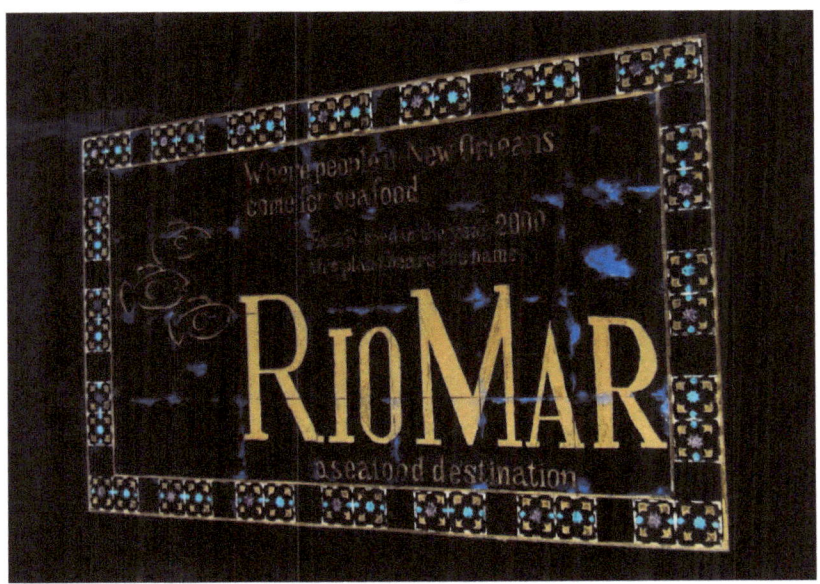

Moistening Time

Rio Mar

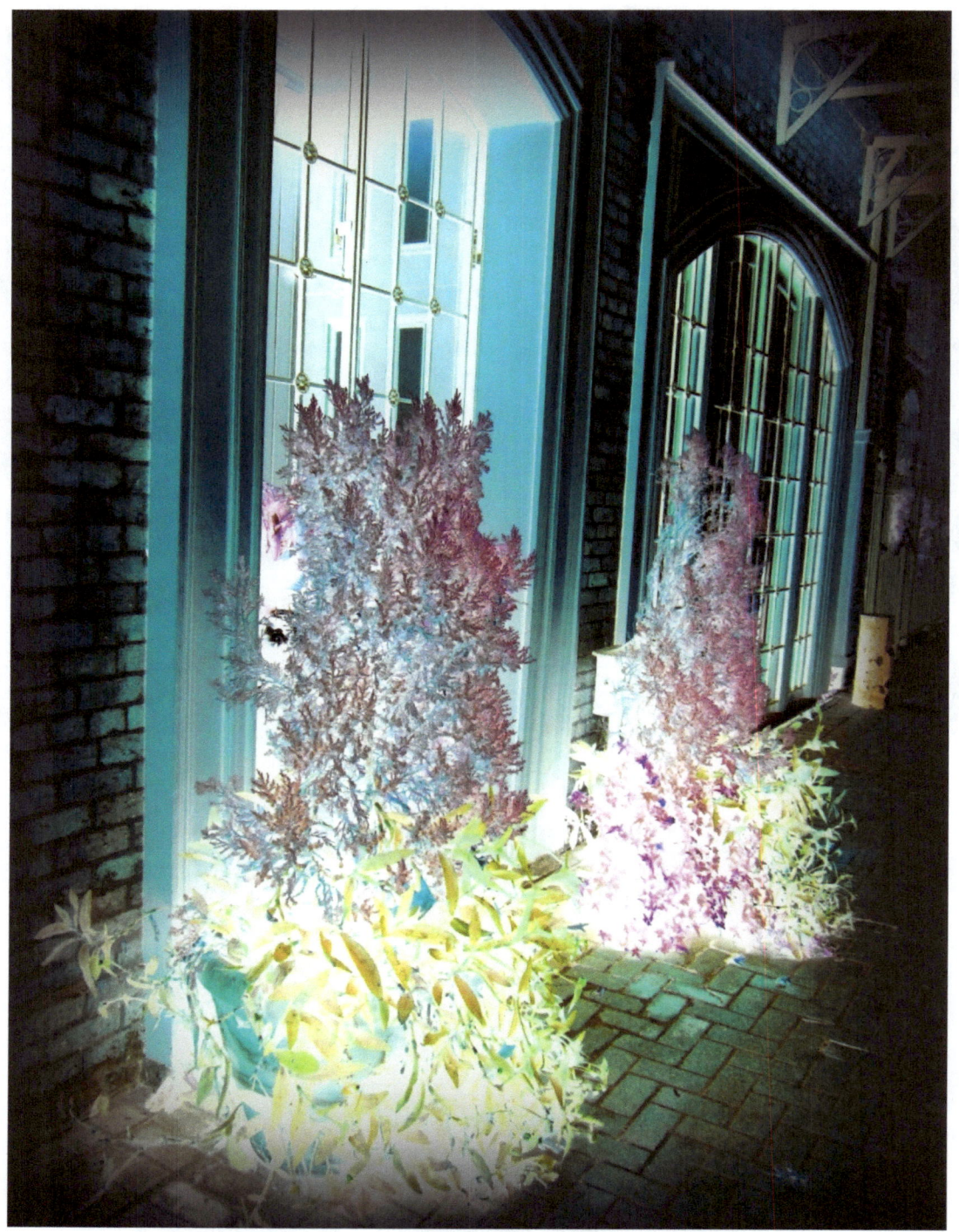

Courtyard II

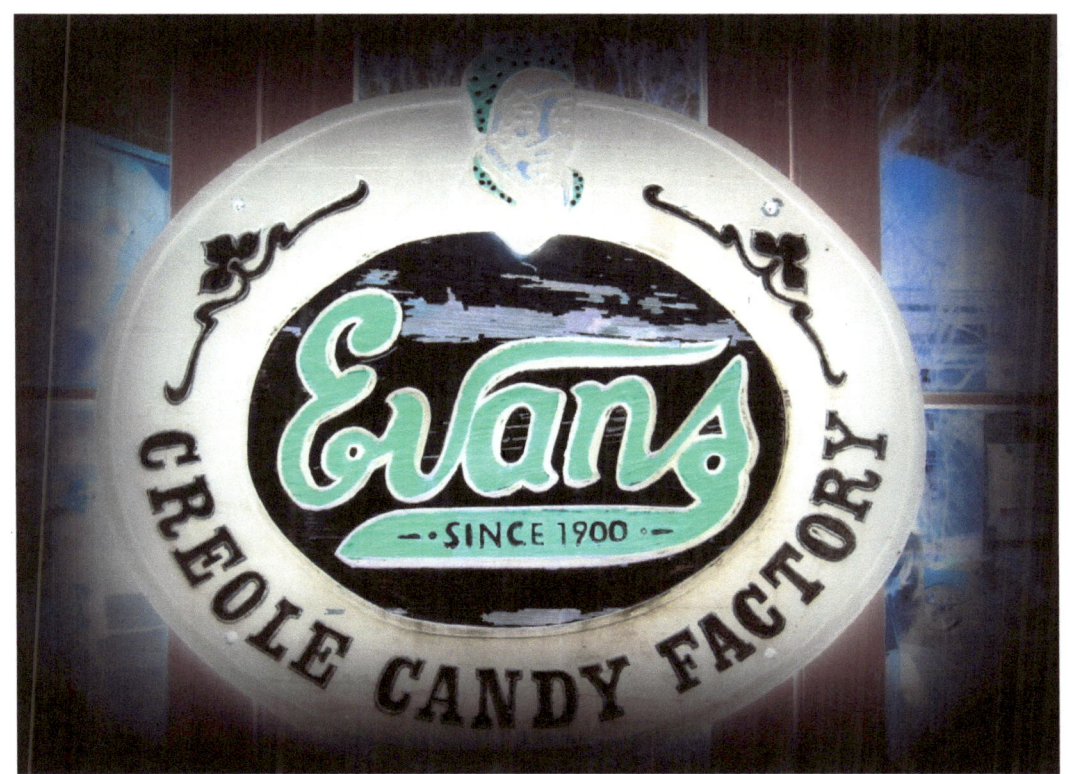

Candyland

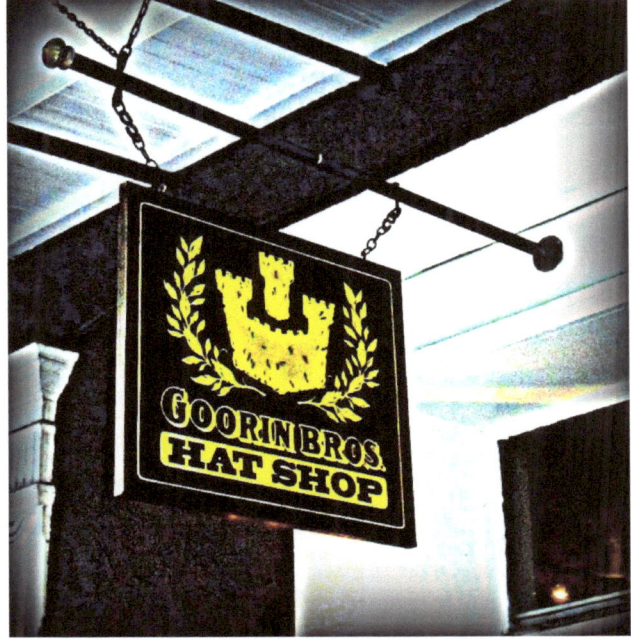

Mad Hatters

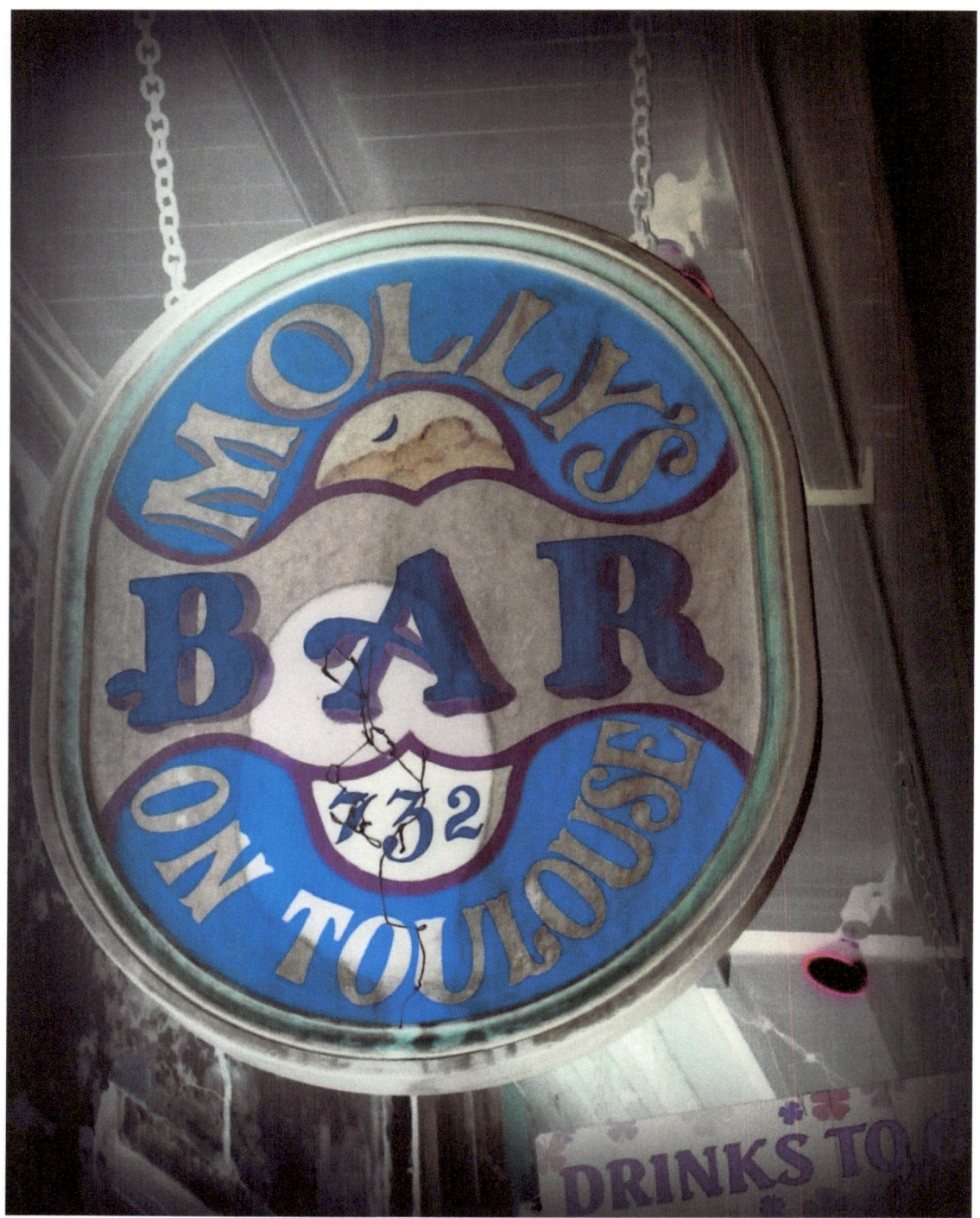

*Good Golly! It's Miss Molly's!*

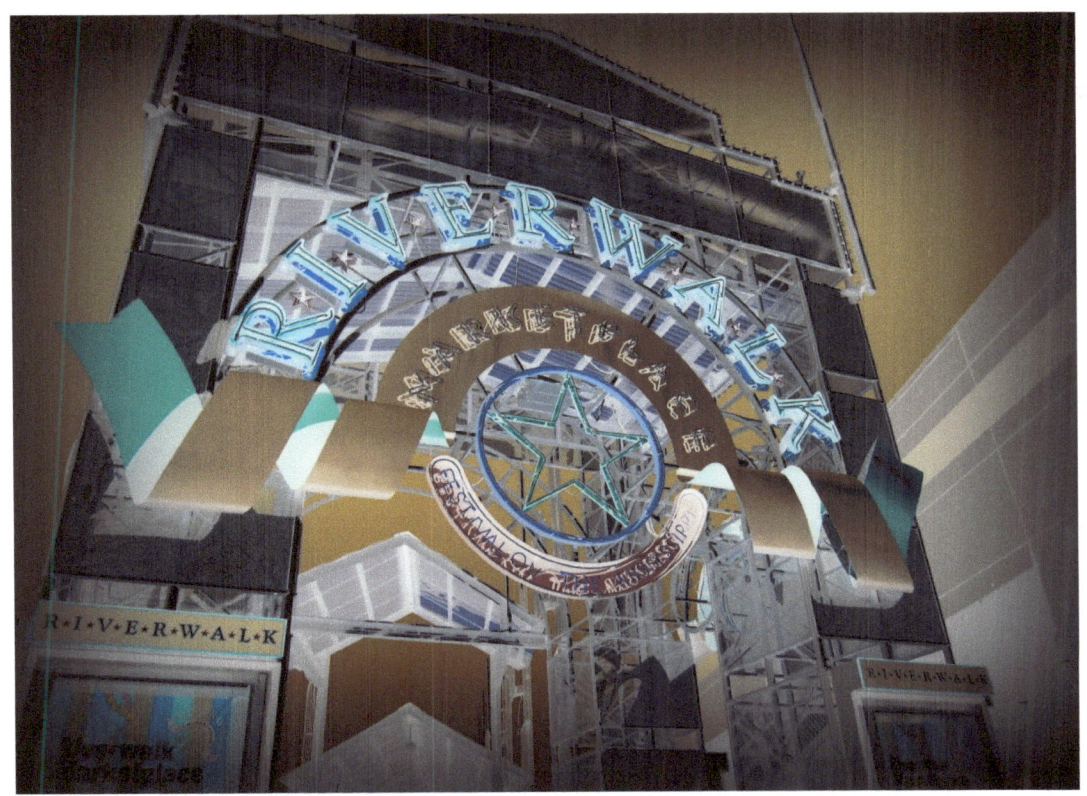

The River Walk

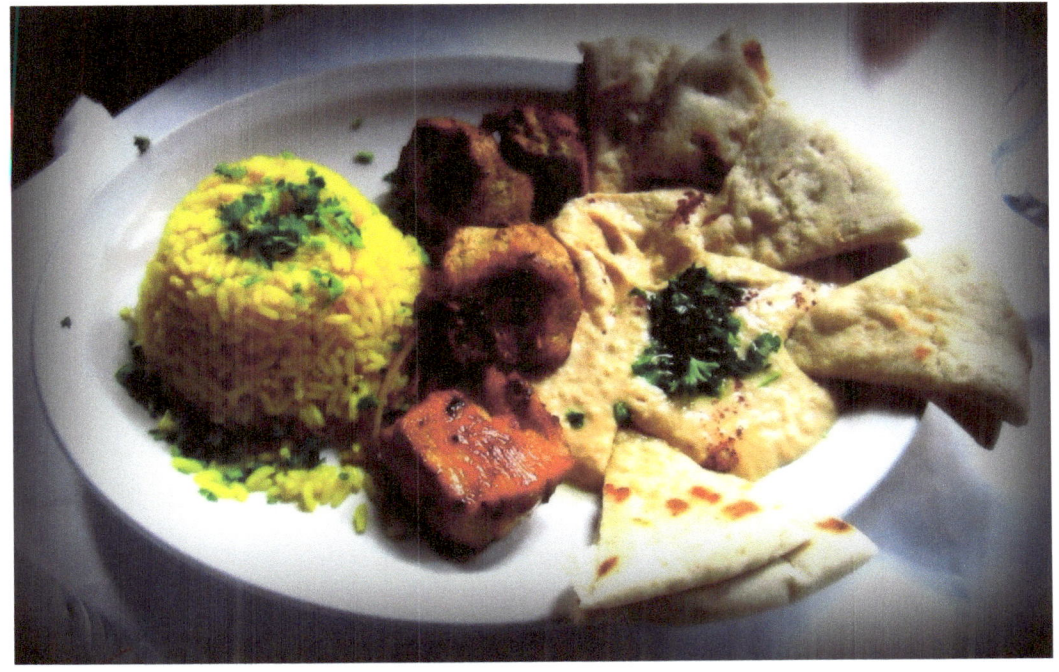

A Little Lunch

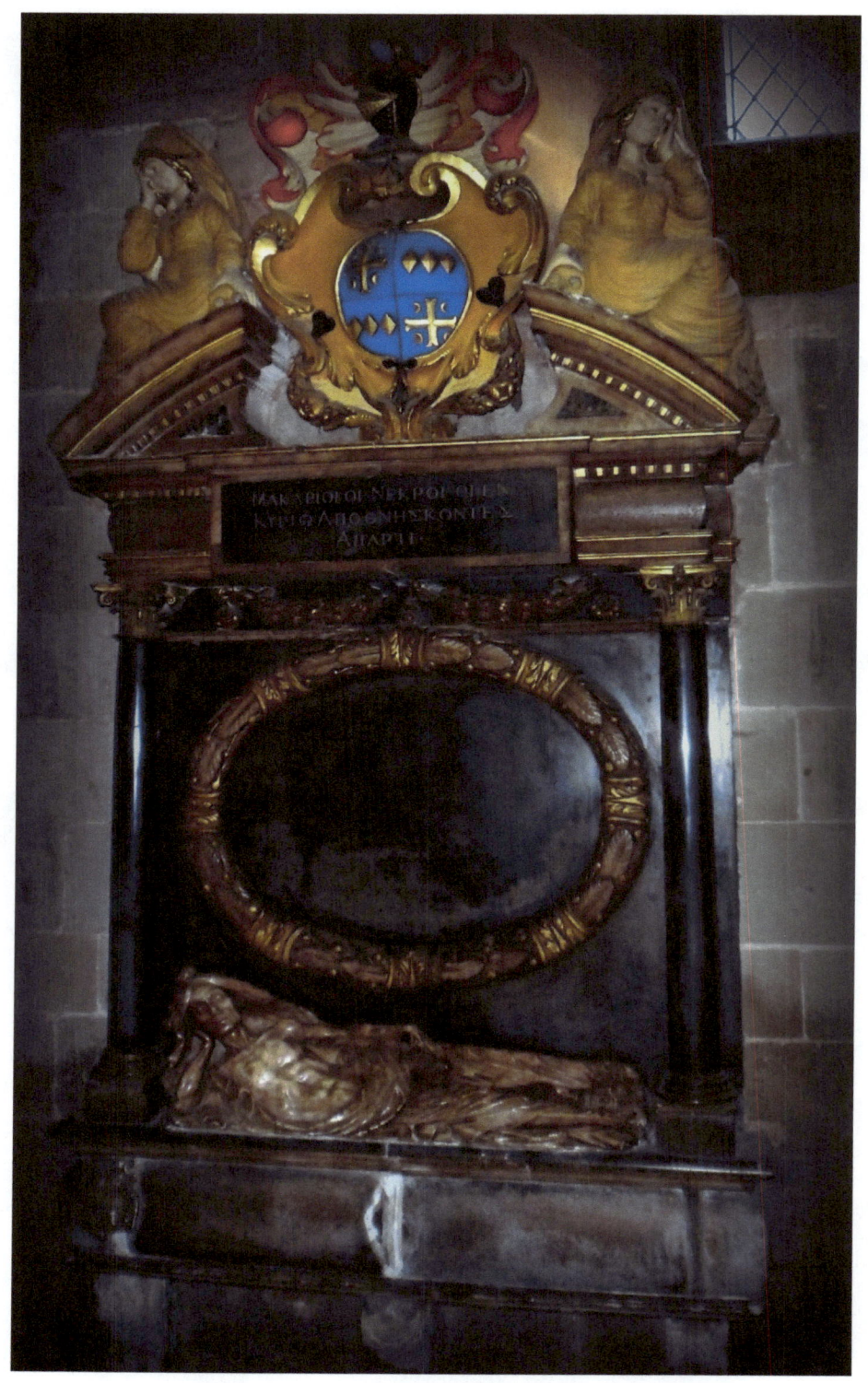

Worcester Cathedral I

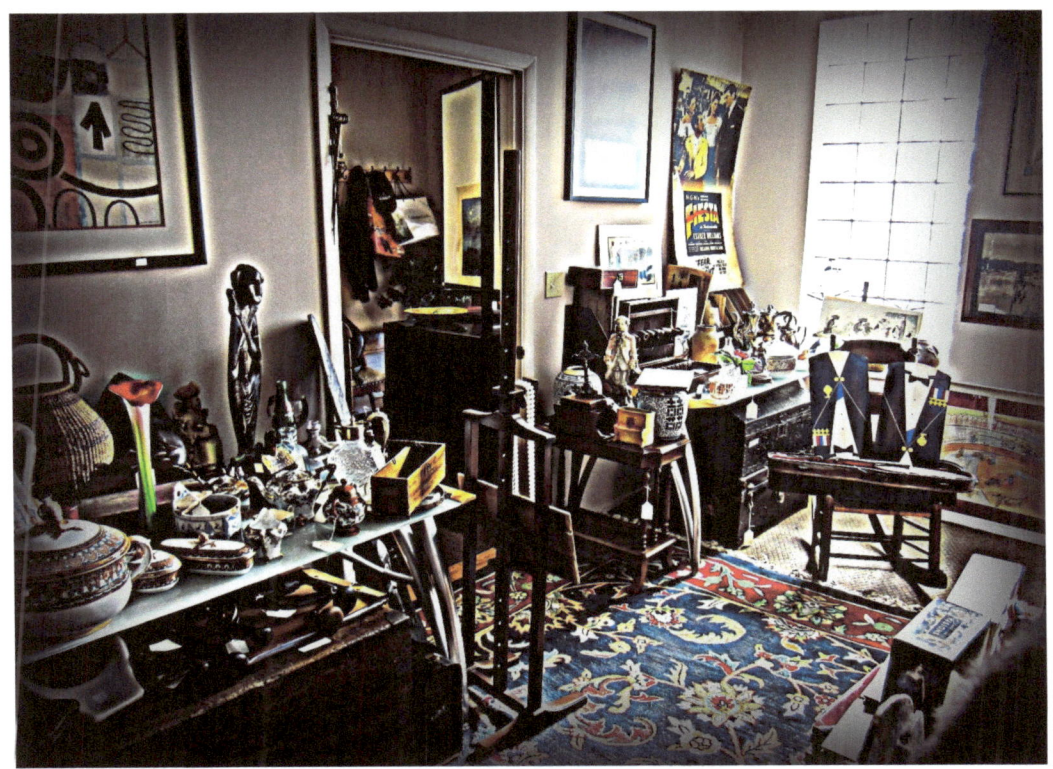

West College Antiques

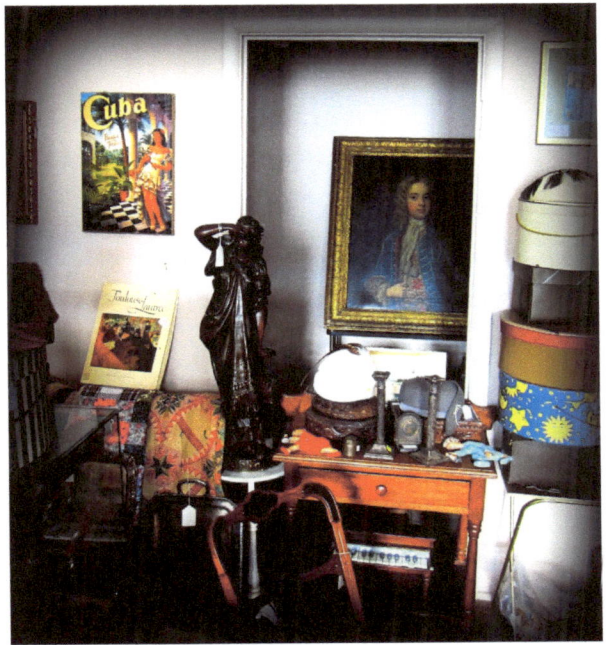

West College Antiques II

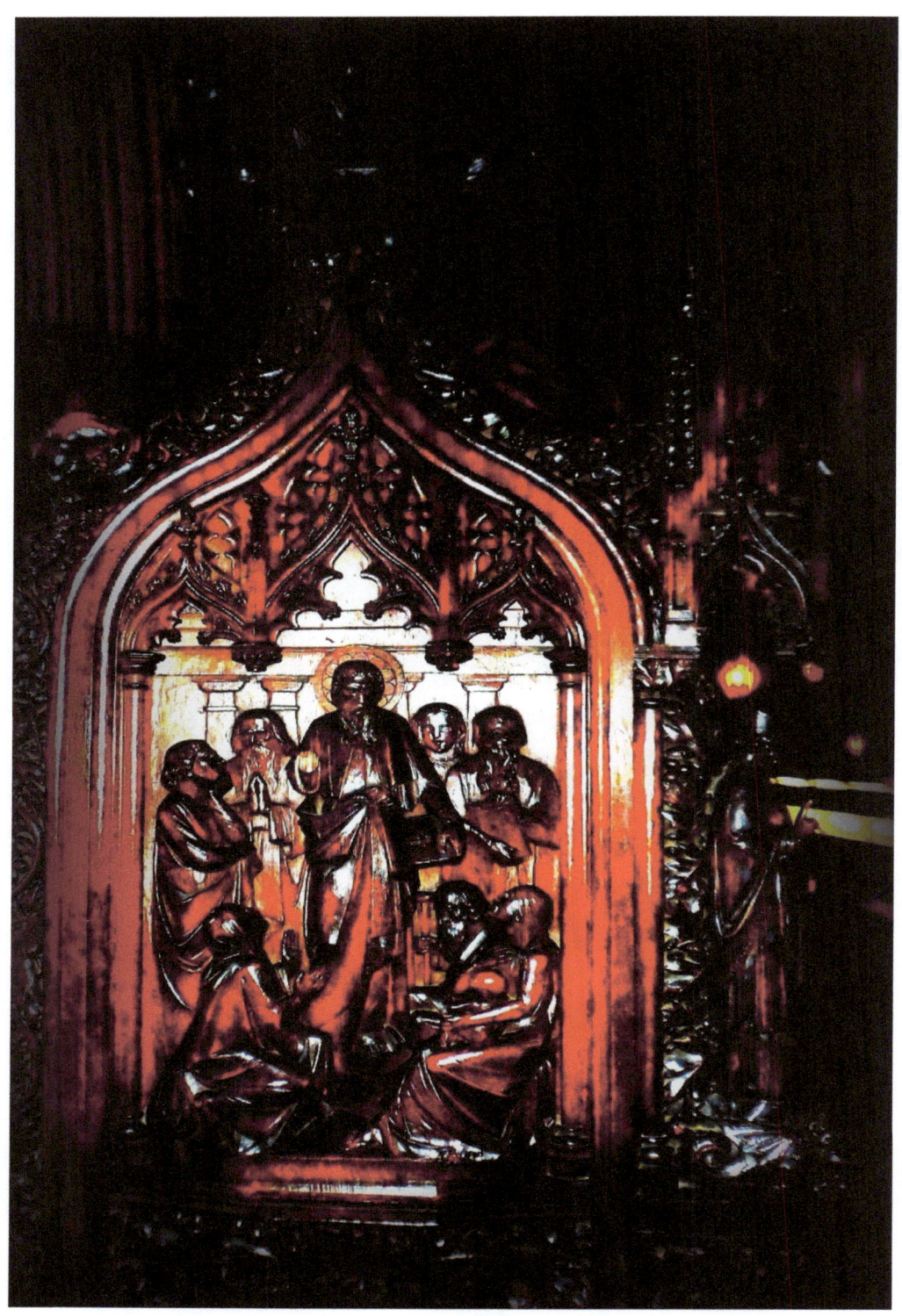

Worcester Cathedral II

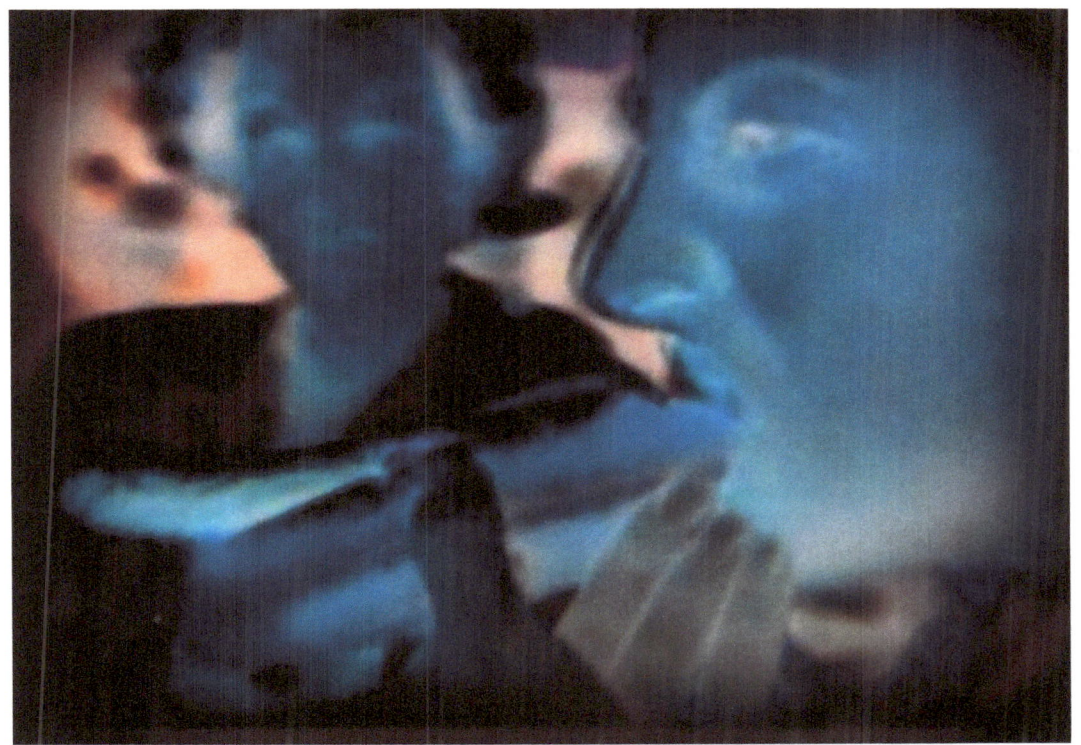

Guzzler

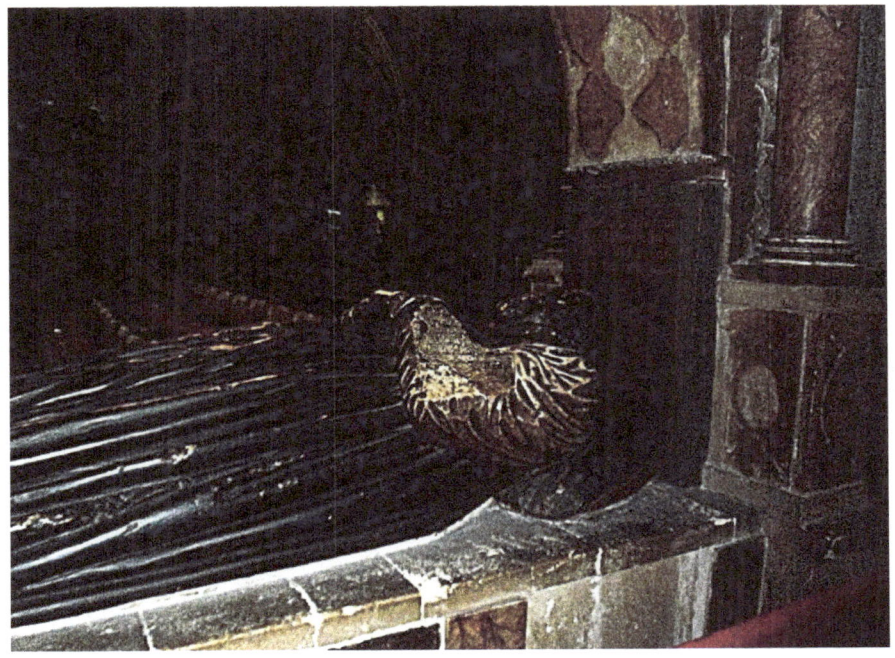

An Over-Guzzled Blur

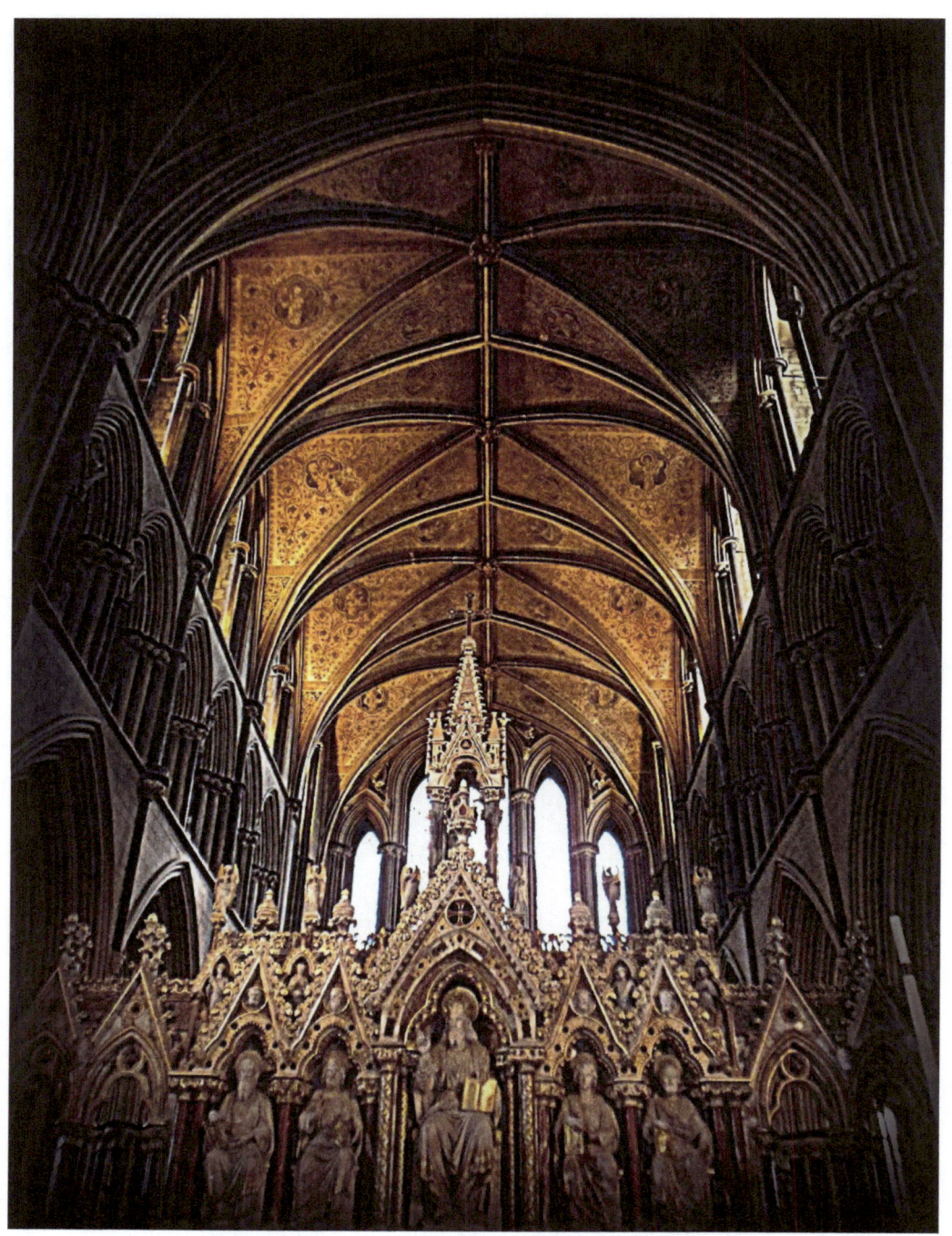

Worcester Cathedral III

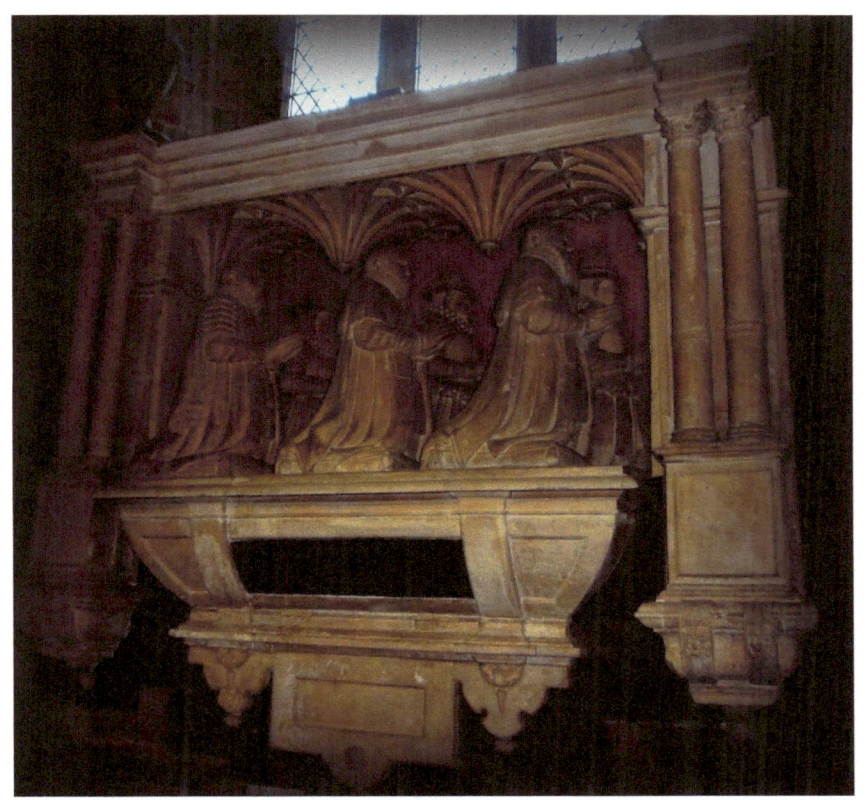

Worcester Cathedral IV

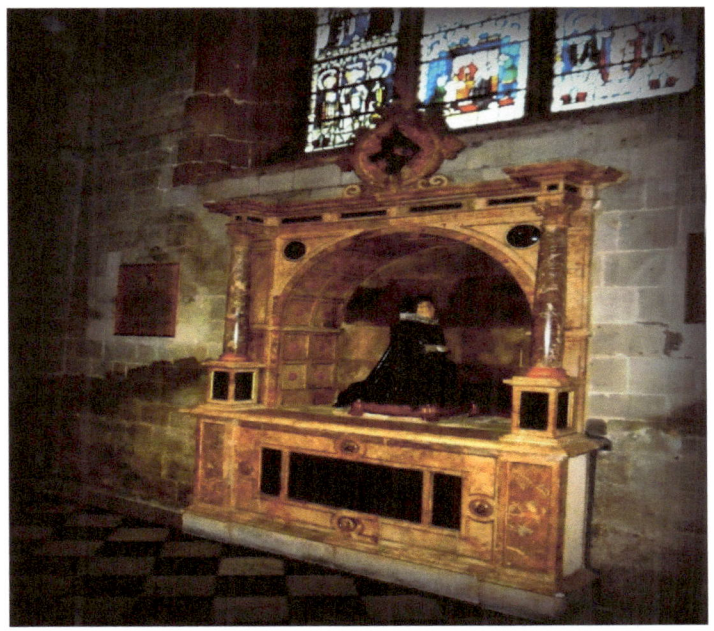

Worcester Cathedral V

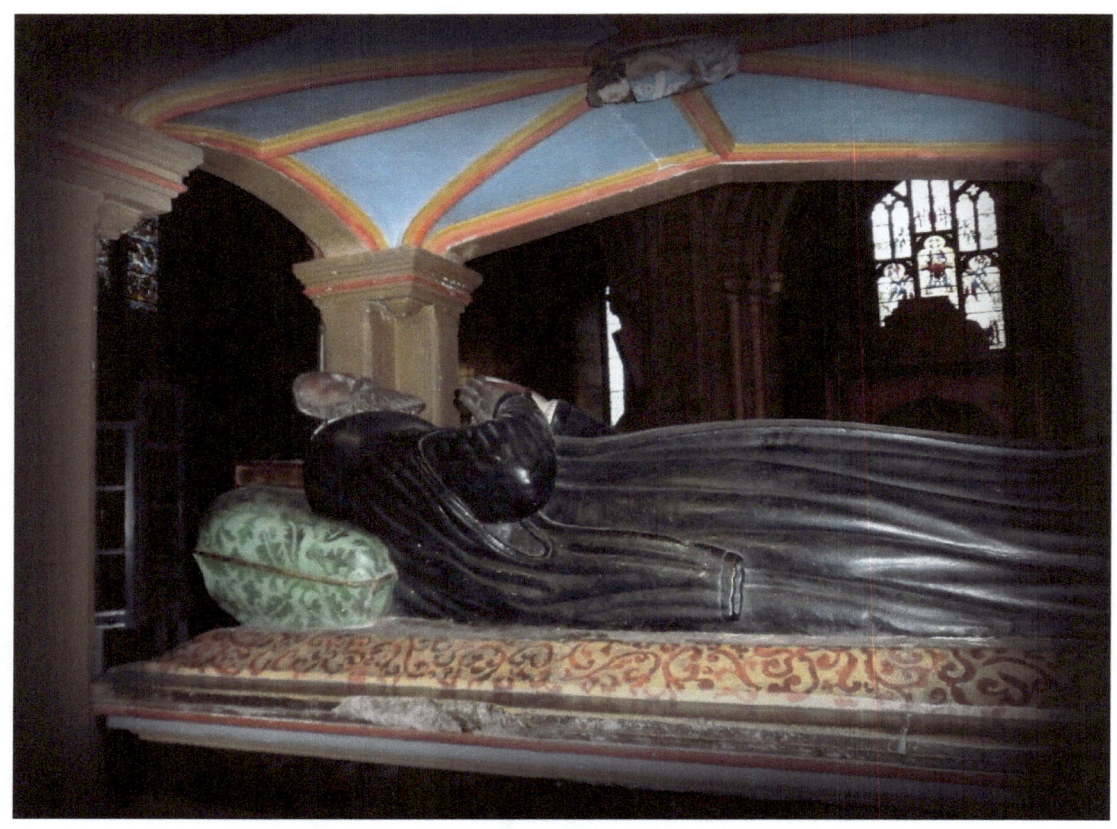

Got Ripped

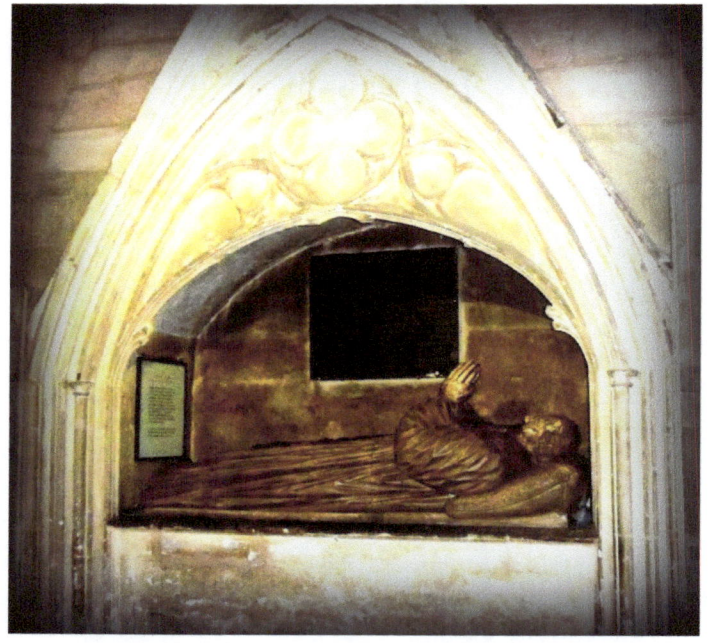

Everyone is Ripped

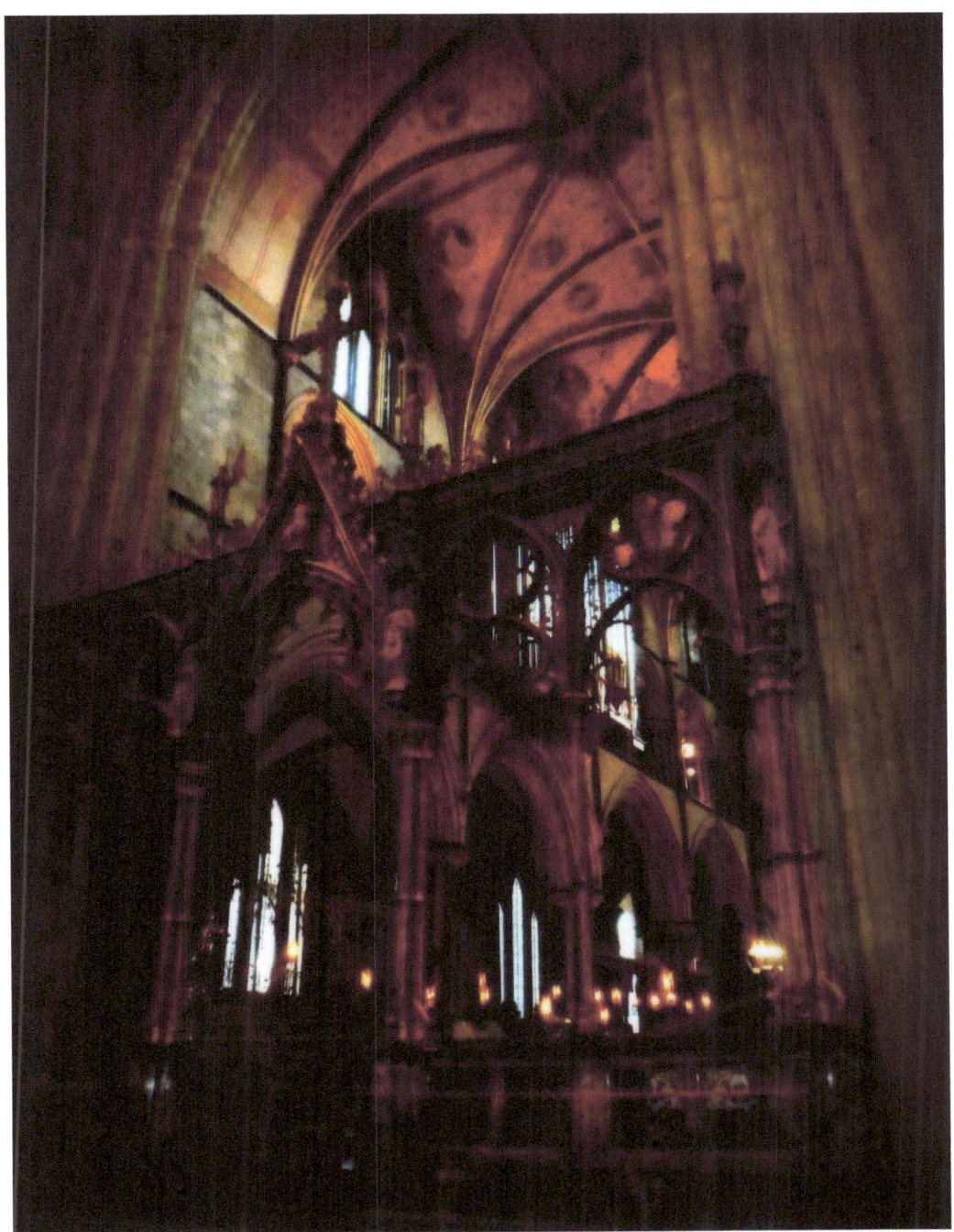

Worcester Cathedral VI

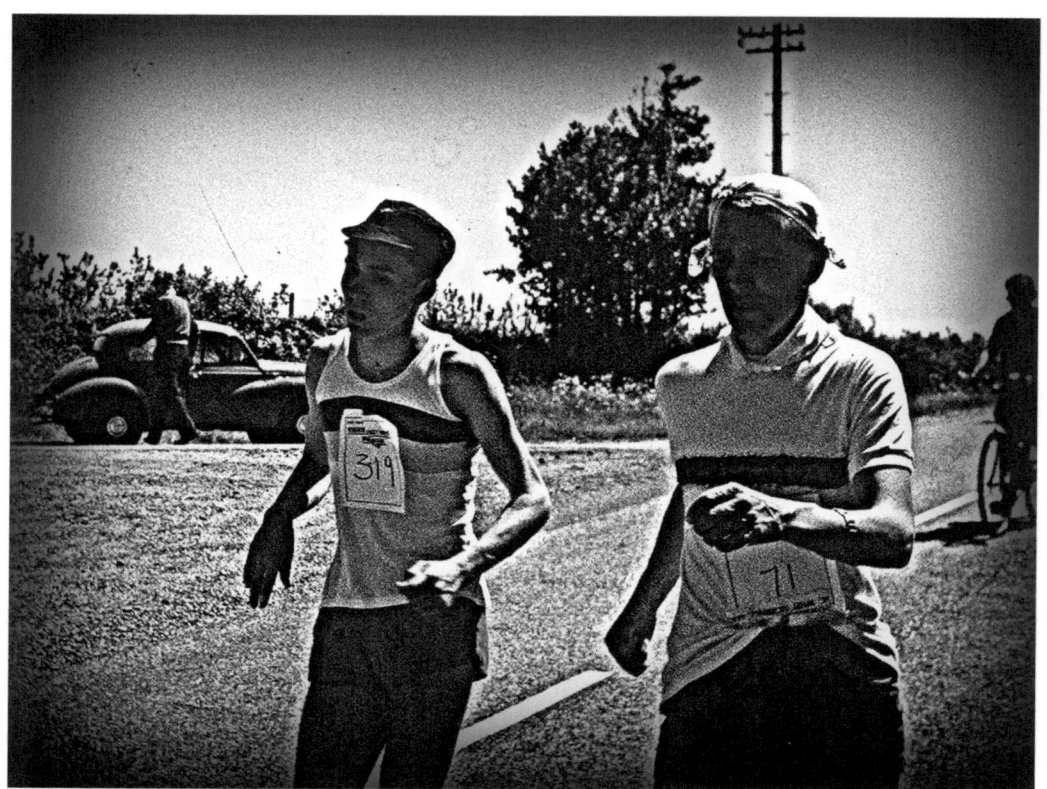

Essex Weekly News Walk 1965 Winners

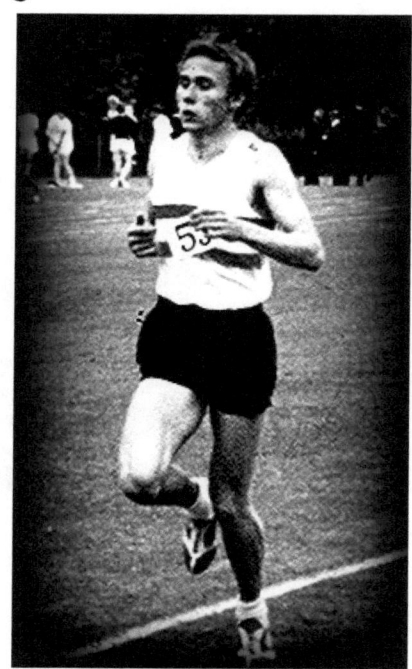

The Miler by A.M.Fowler

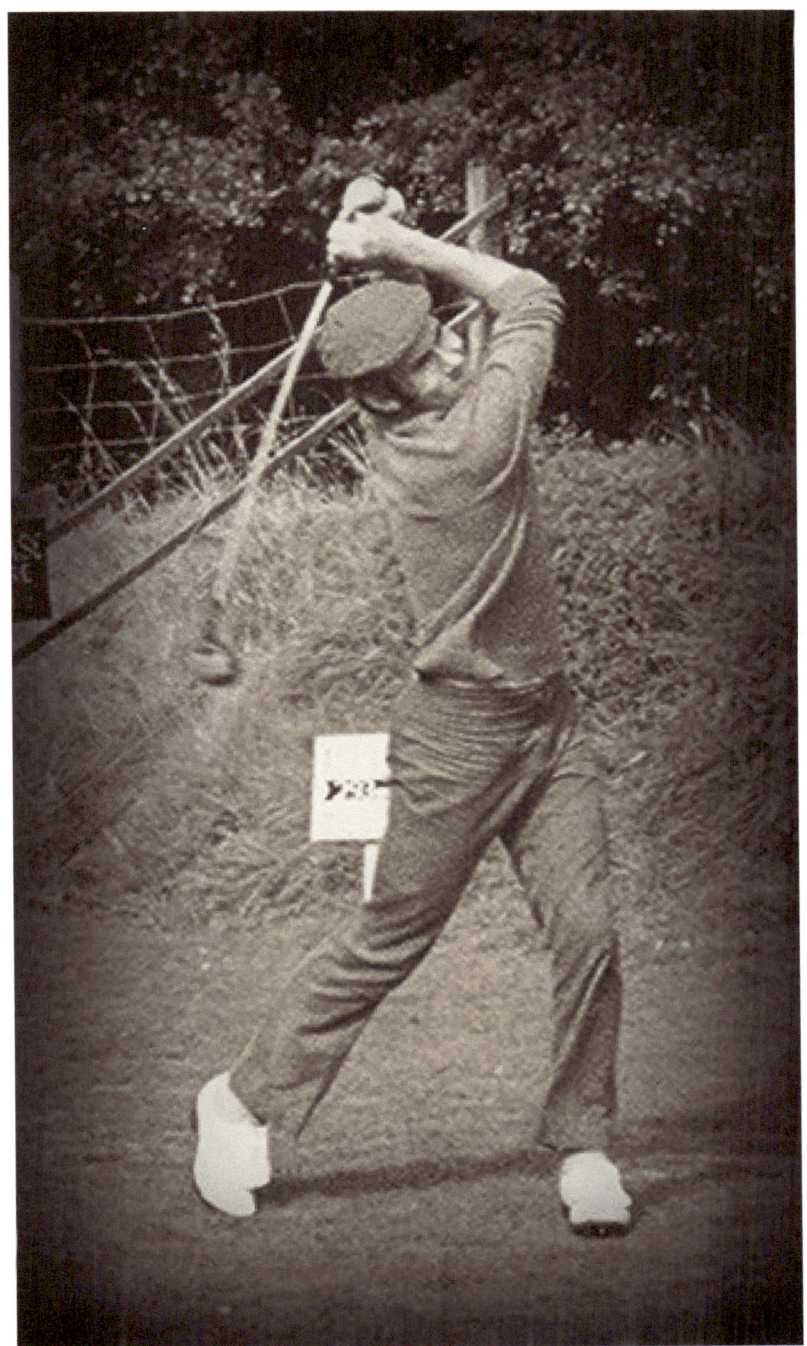

Swing Time in 1967 by A. M. Fowler

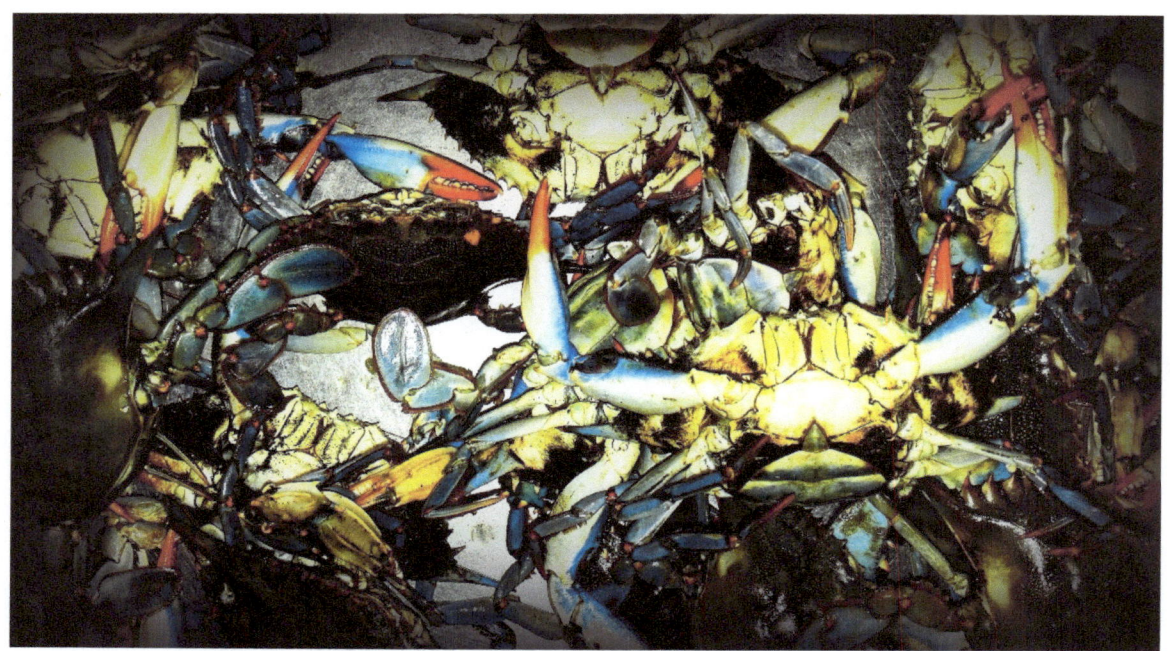

The Blue Crab Ball

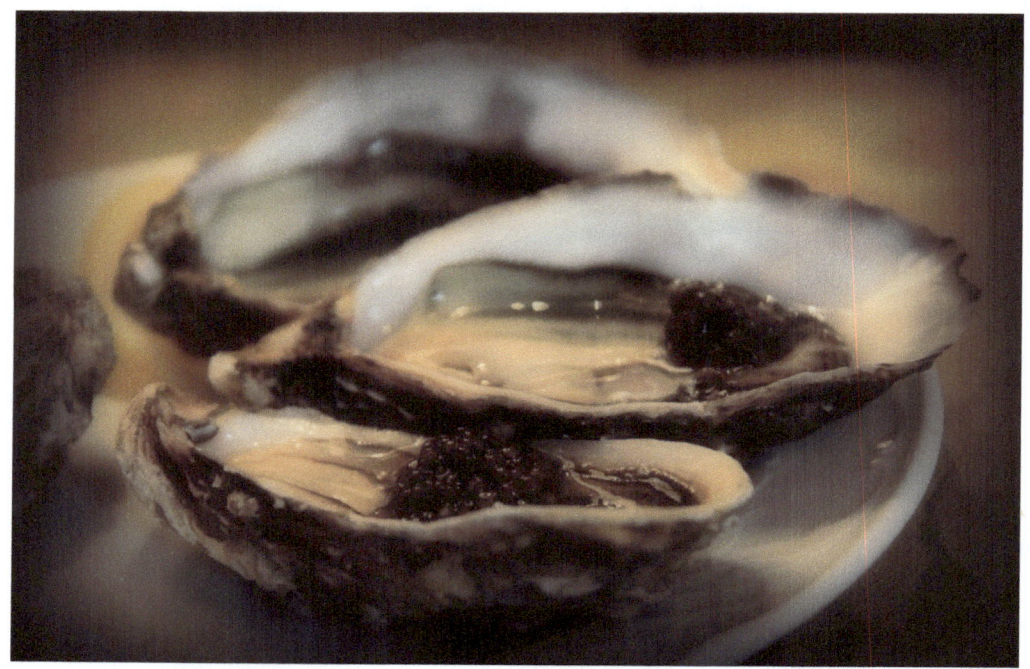

Naughty...but Nice

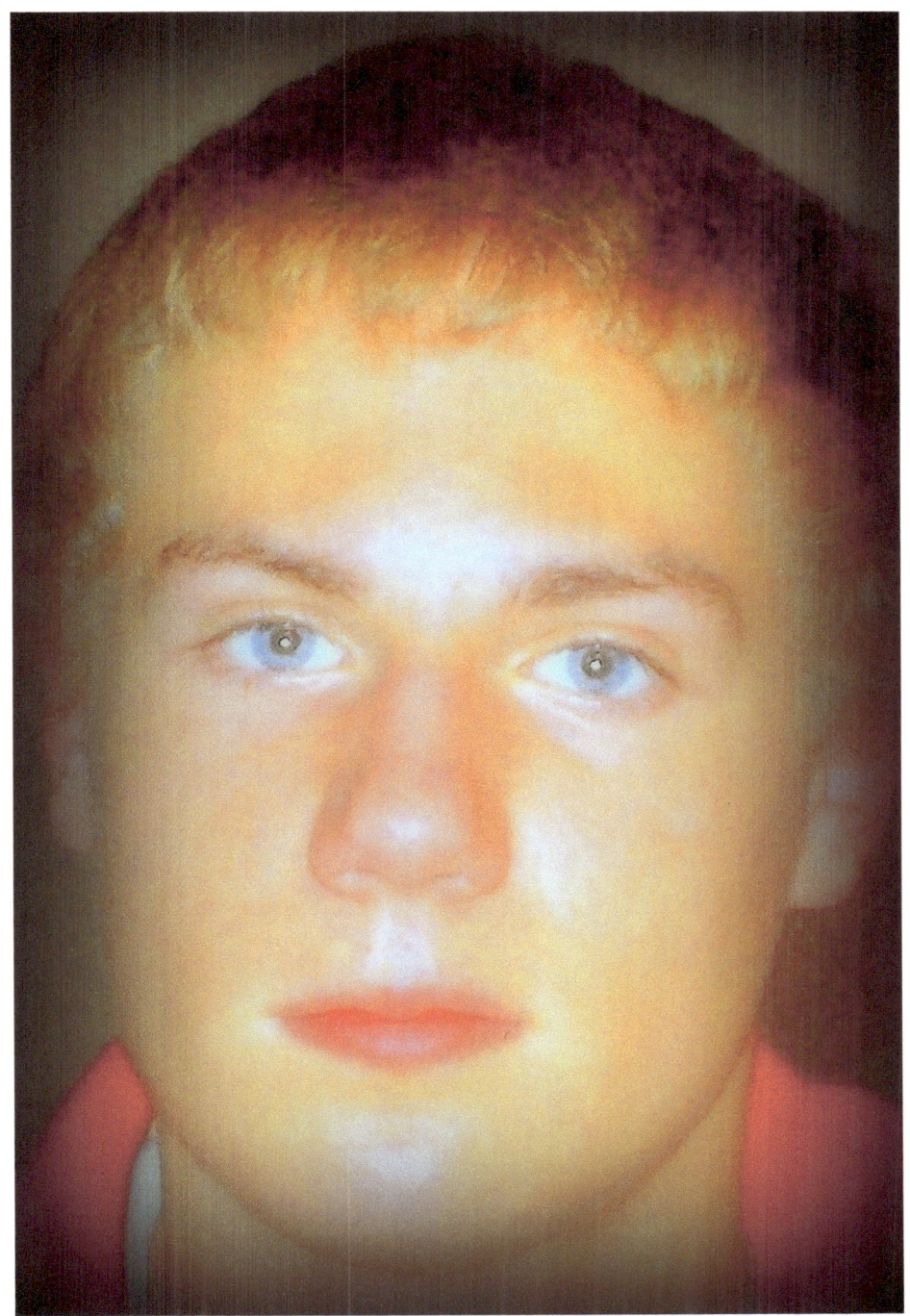

Jelly-Boy Pinky

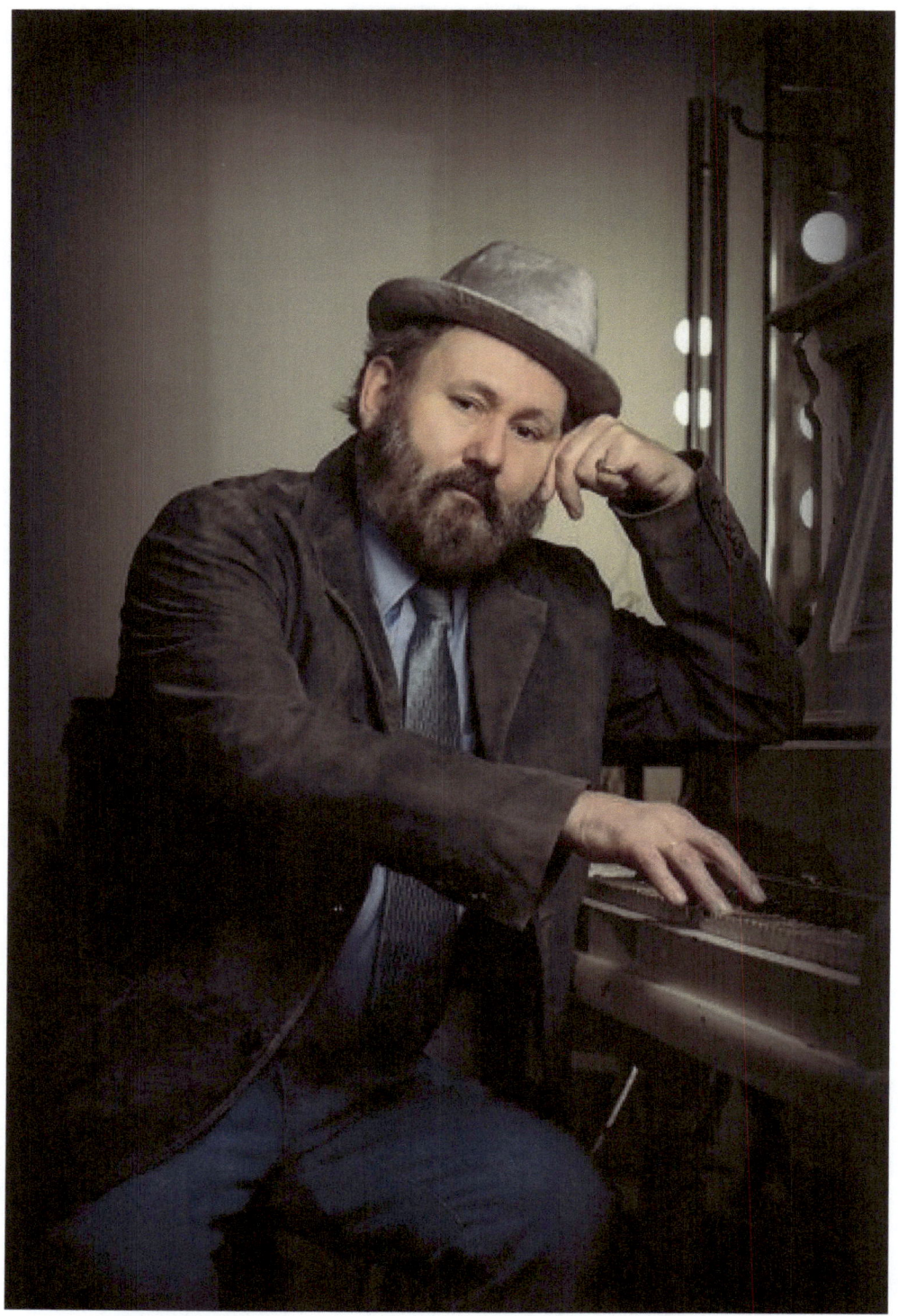

The Old Curmudgeon by Wes

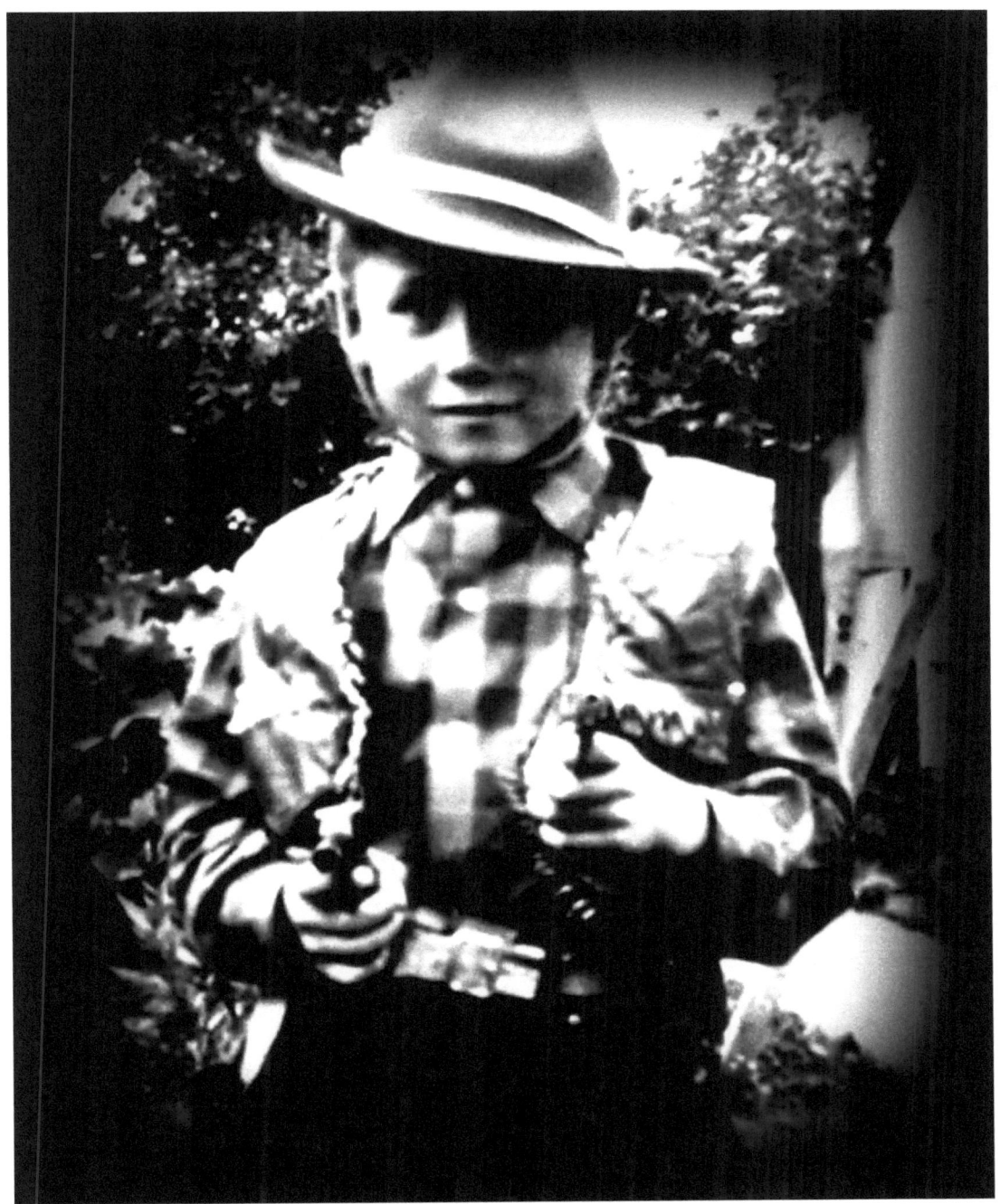

The Cumberland Kid by A. M. Fowler

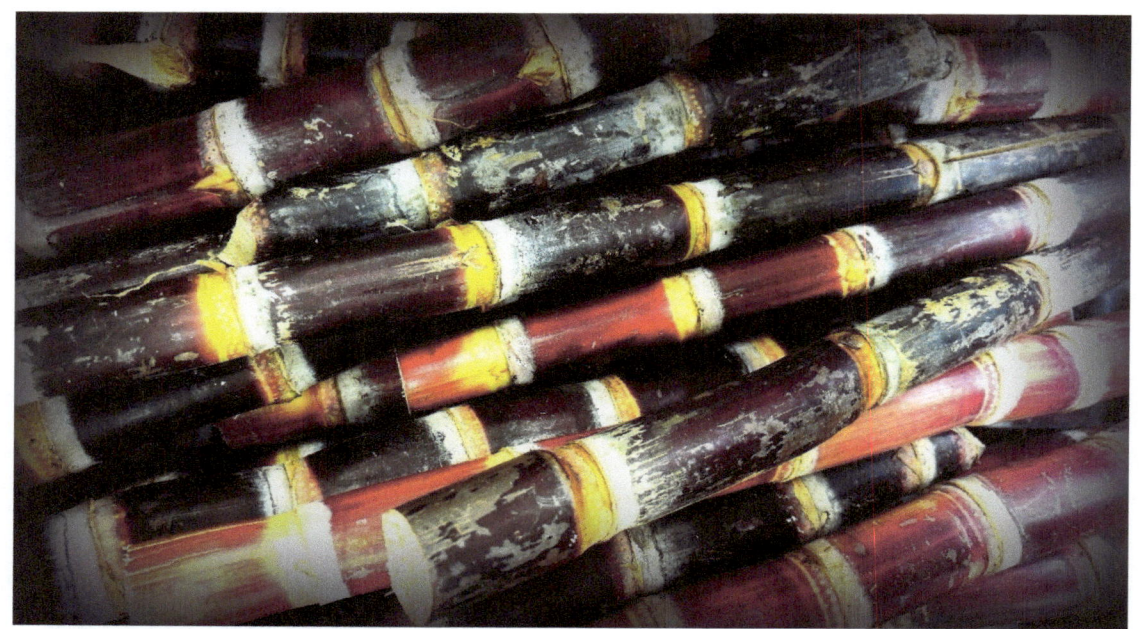

The Bamboo Curtain

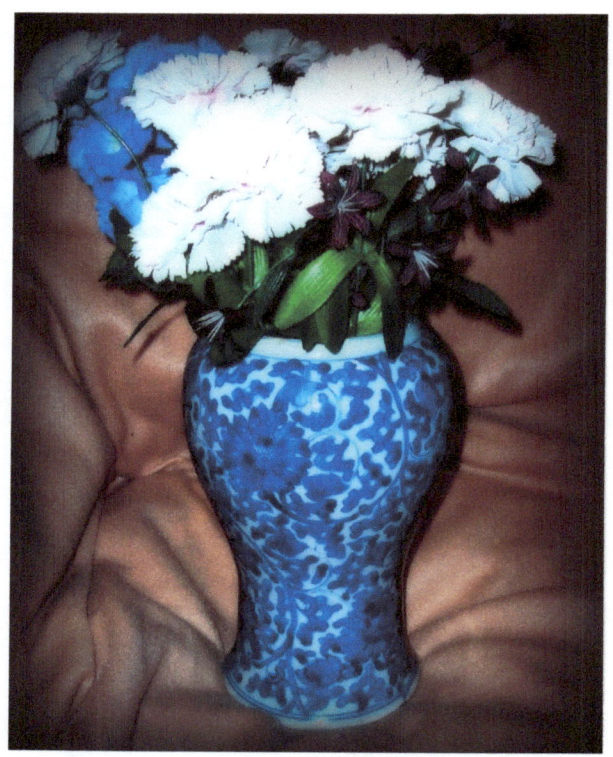

Ming Dynasty Vase

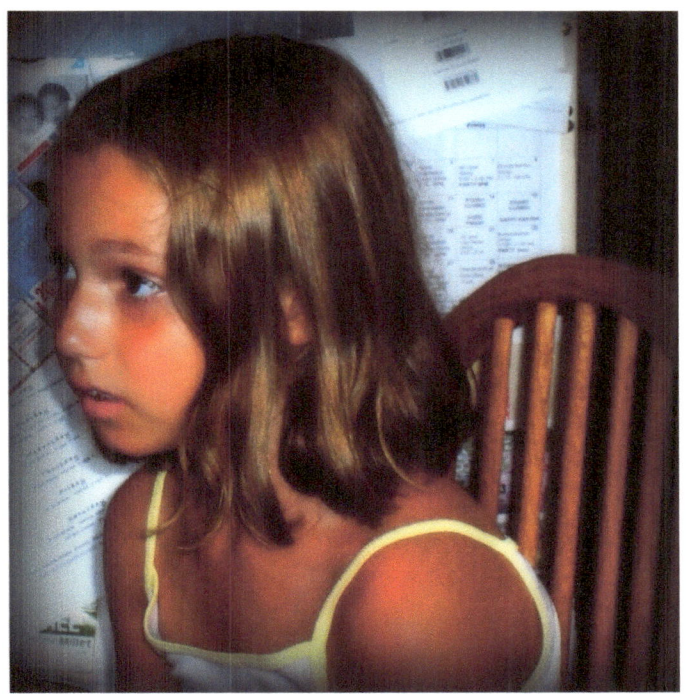

Alex

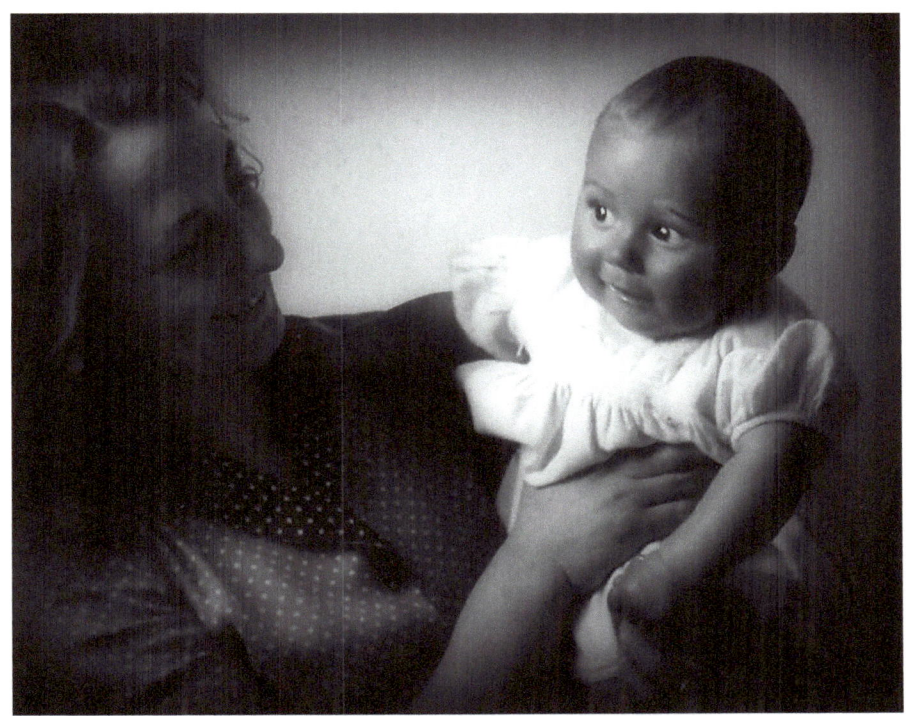

Kid with a Big Head by A. M. Fowler 1950

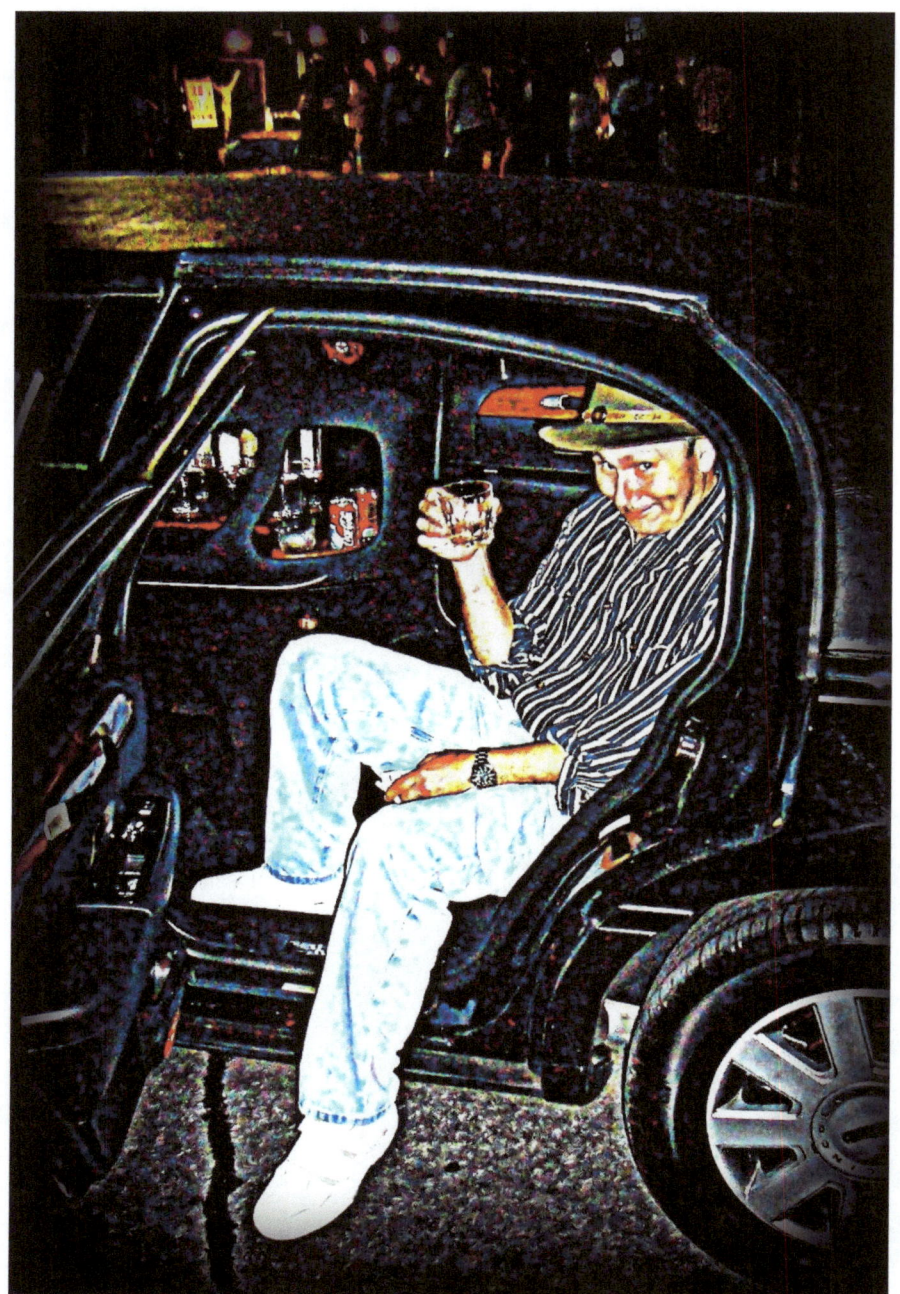

Inebriated Comedian in Austin,Texas
Playing The Velveeta Room

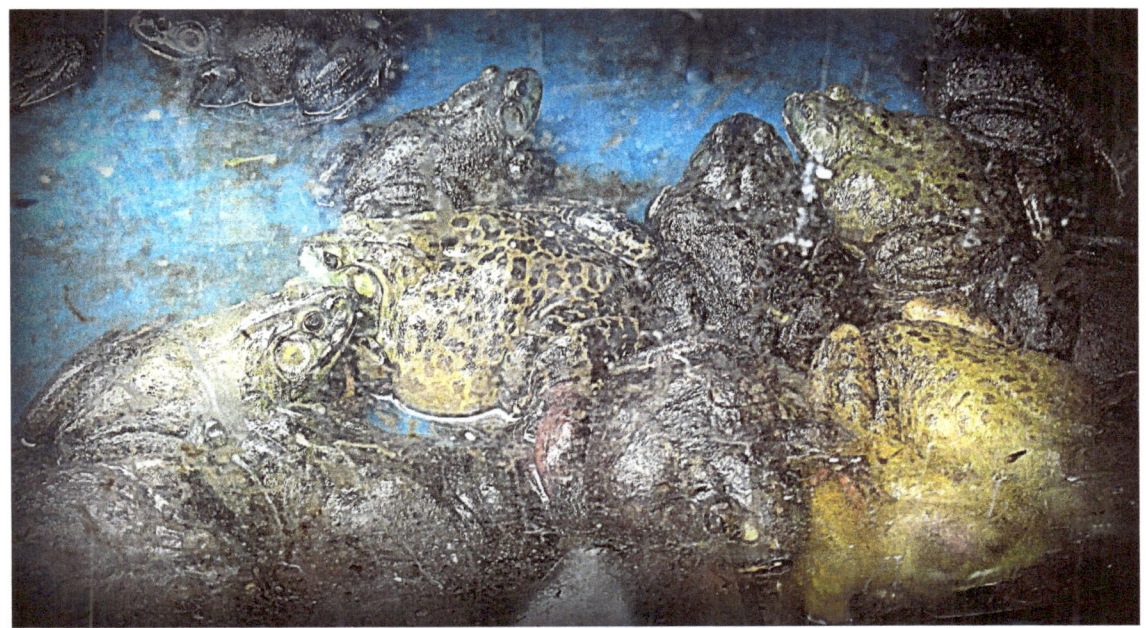

Frog Philosophers

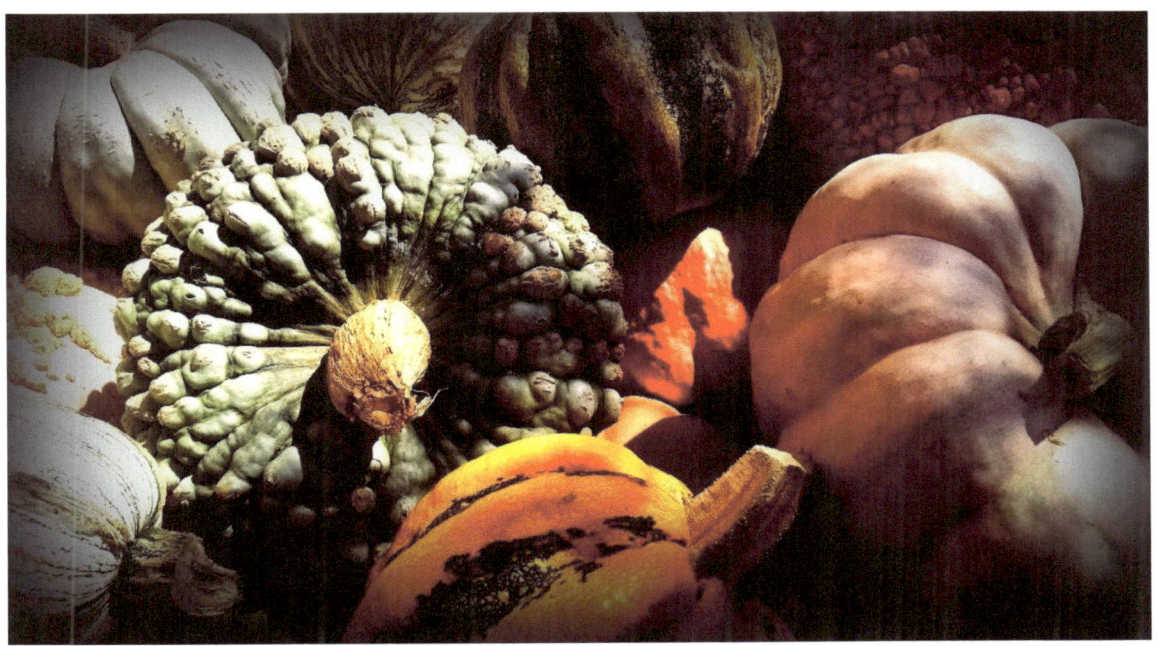

Mutant Gourds

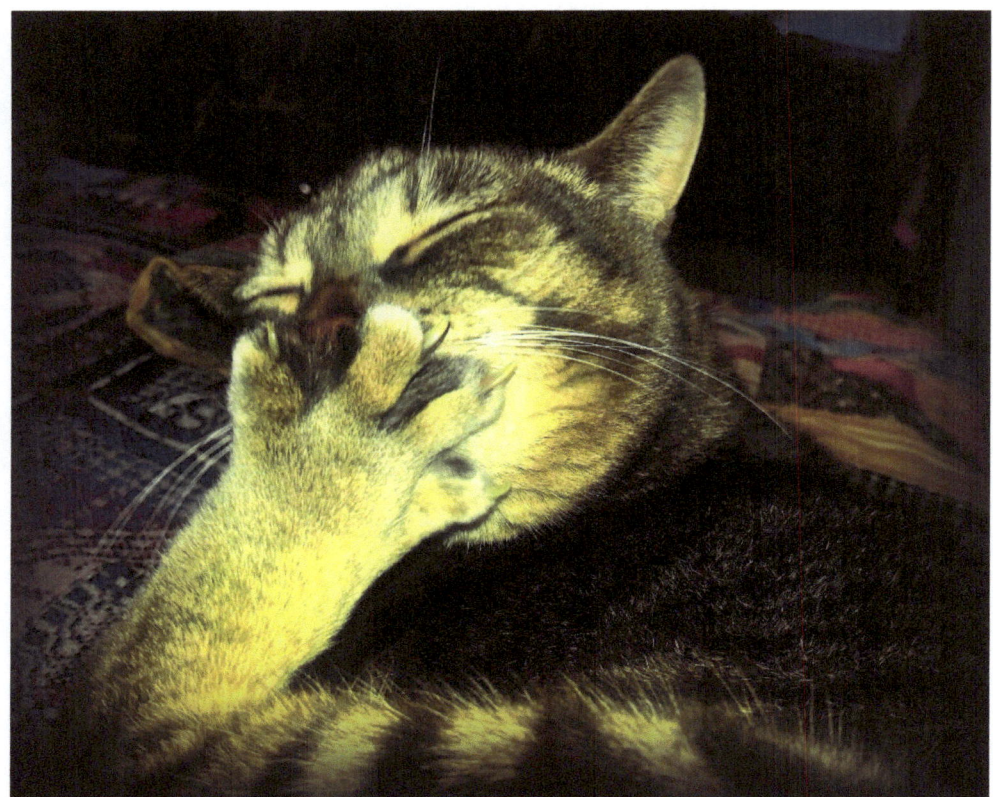

Mrs. Luna Slocombe

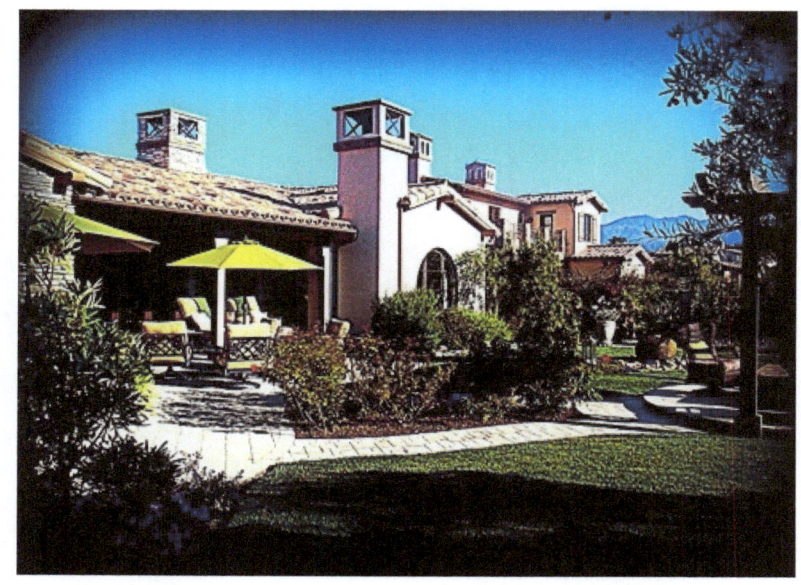

Splendid Home in California

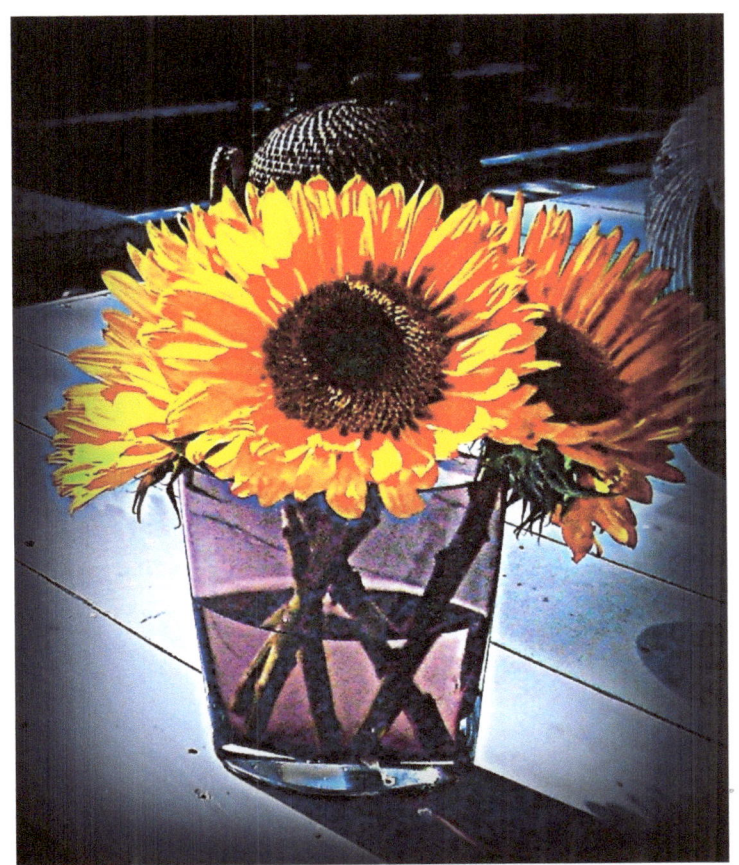

The Other Sunflowers II

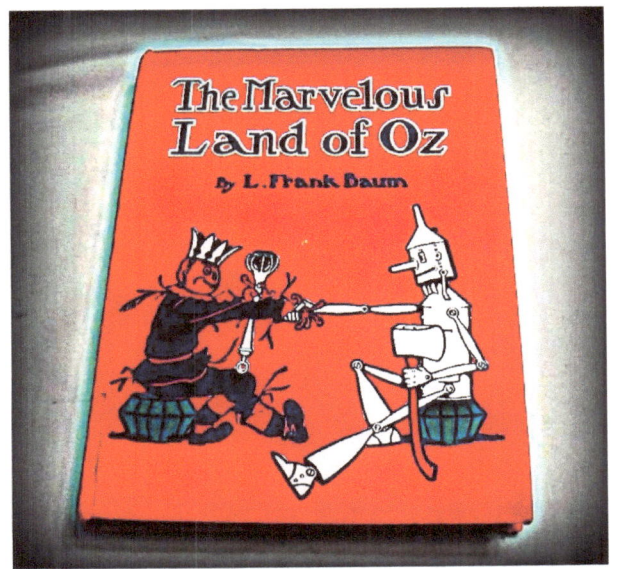

A Wizard Ruse

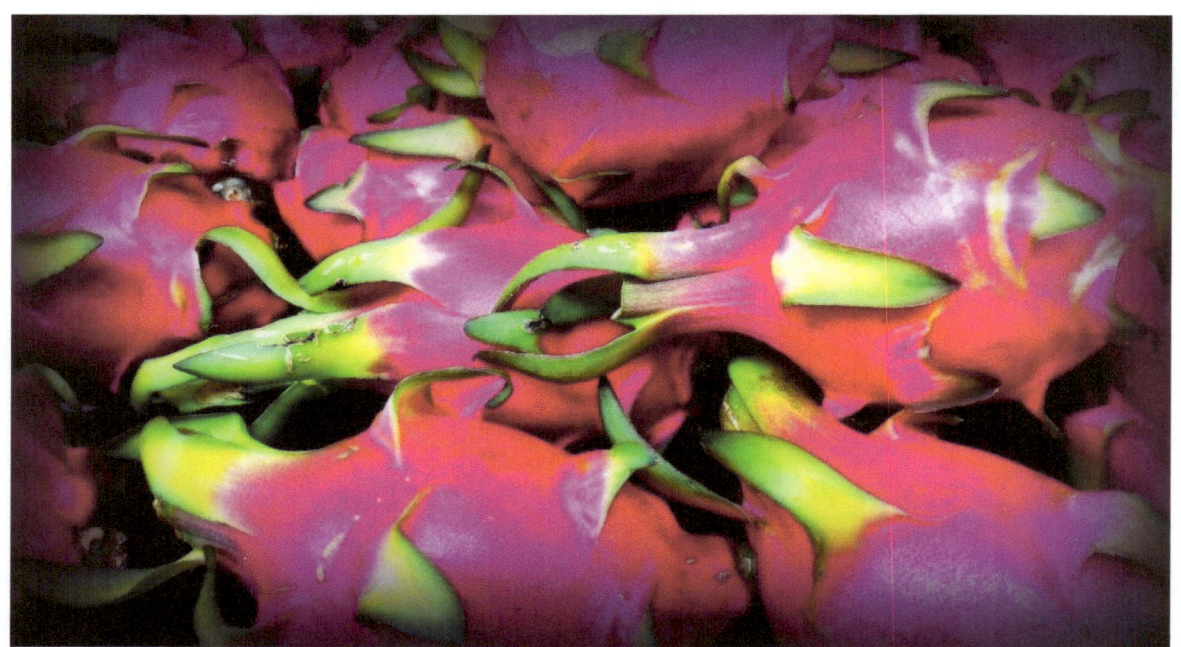

Dragon Fruit of the Loom

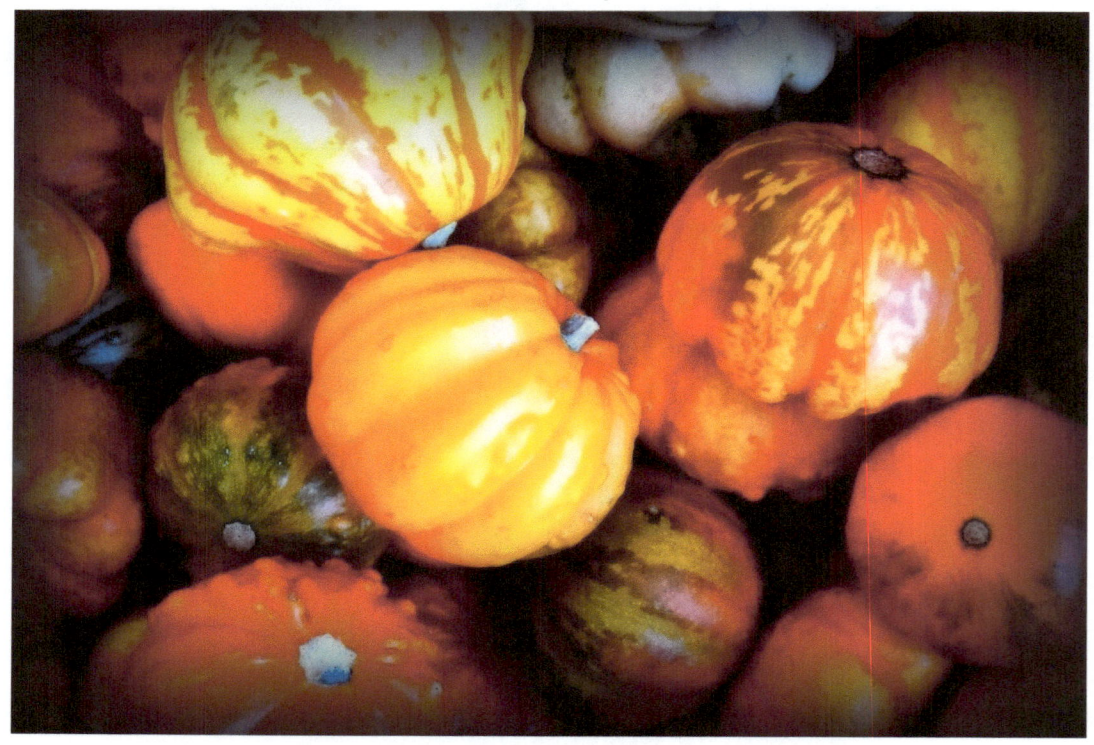

Oh my Gourd!

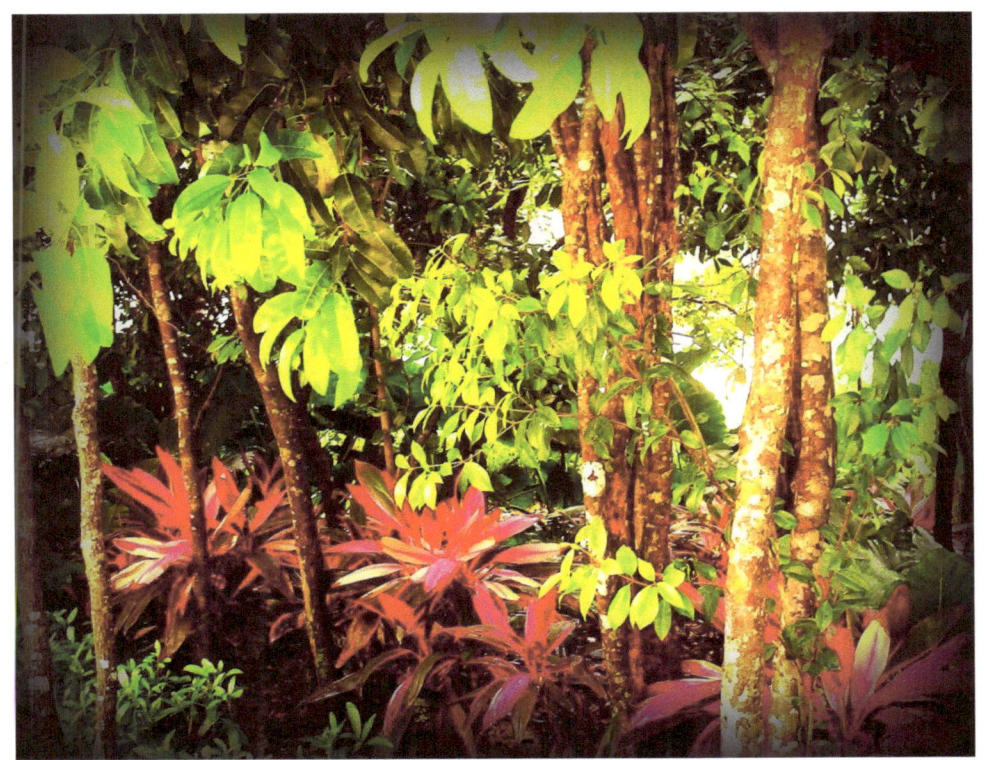

Not Forest Gump

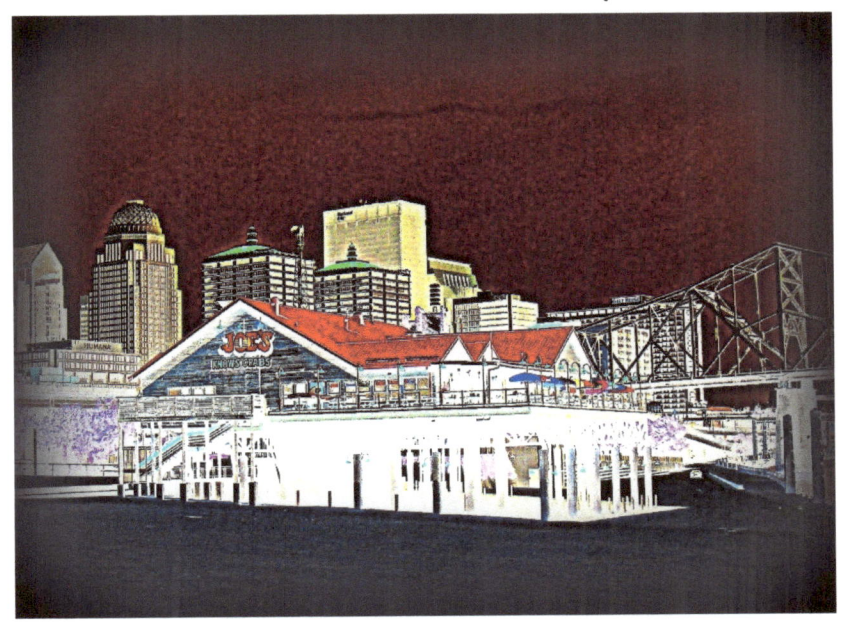

St. Louis – Crab Shack

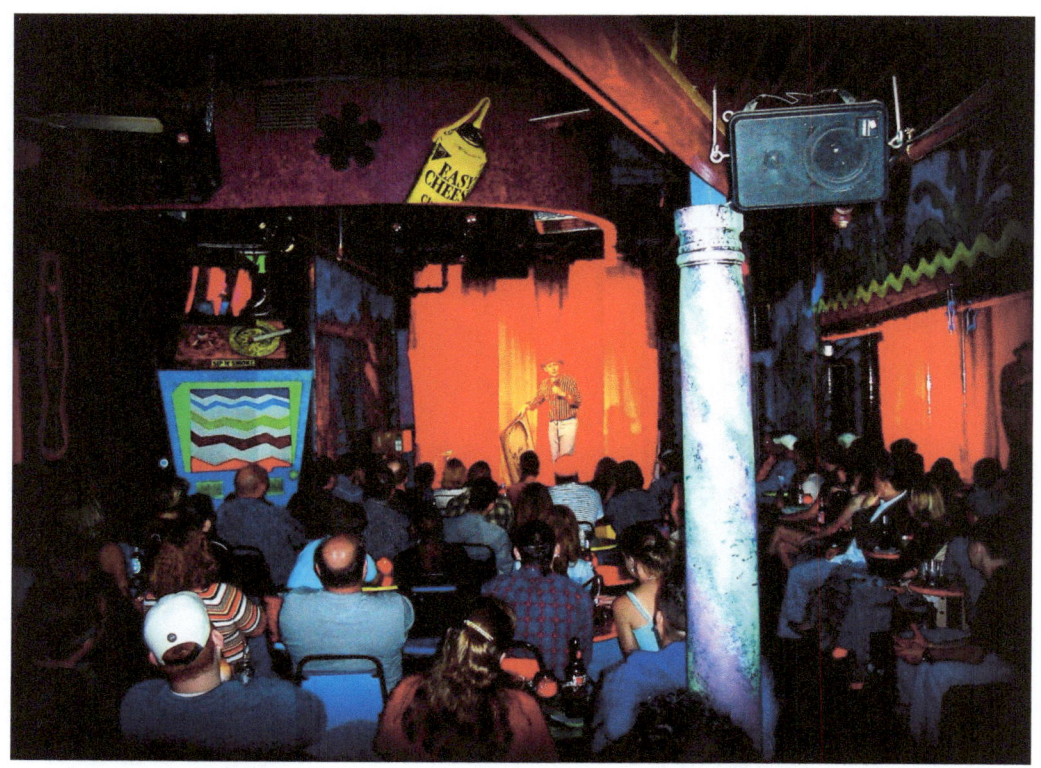

Velveeta Room, Austin, Texas by Joey Waldon

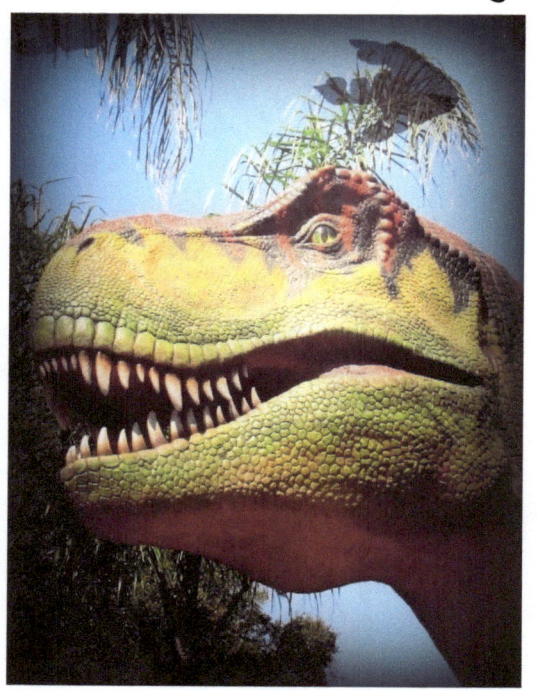

Once Bitten Twice Shy

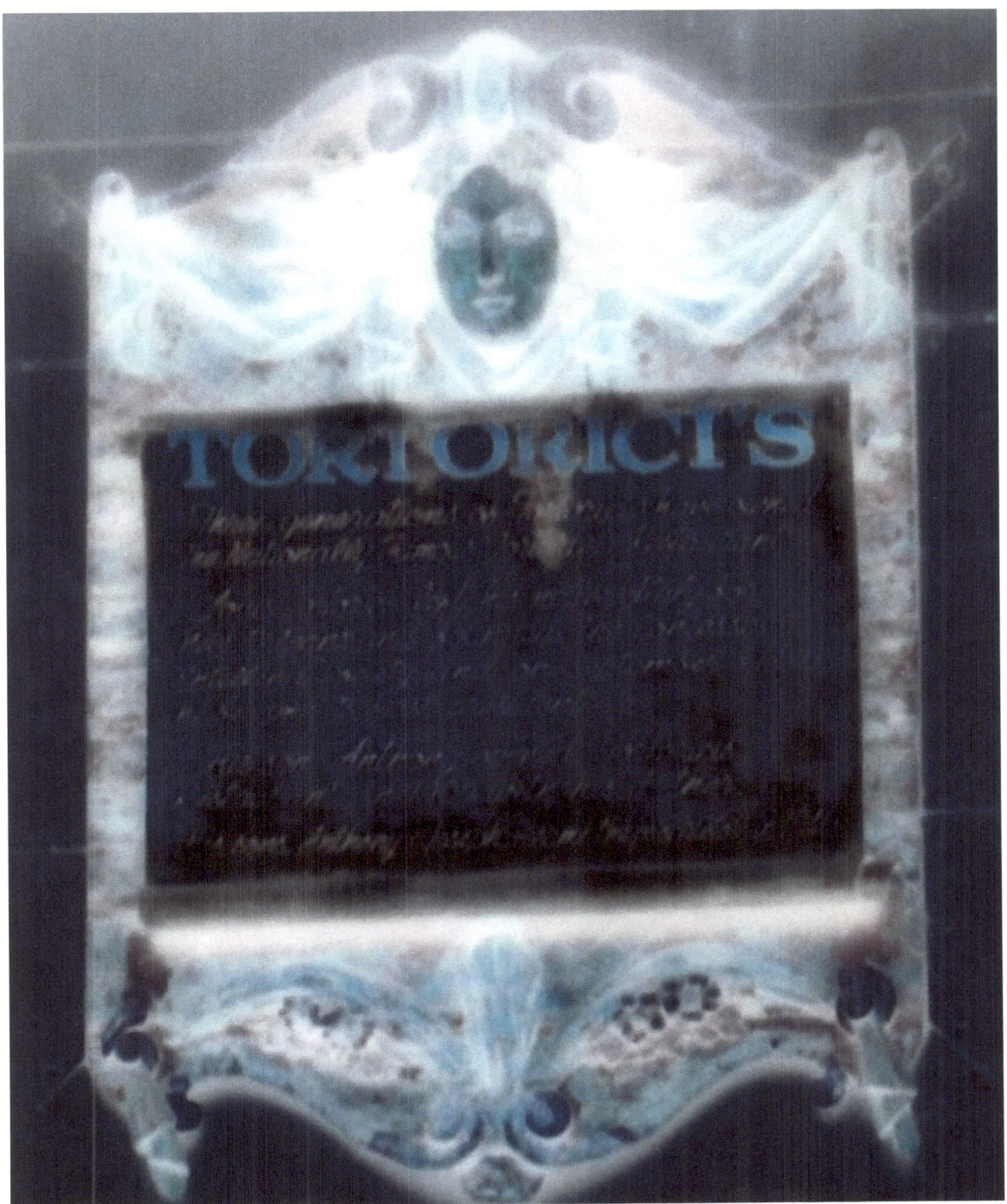

Ethereal Art Nouveau Lady

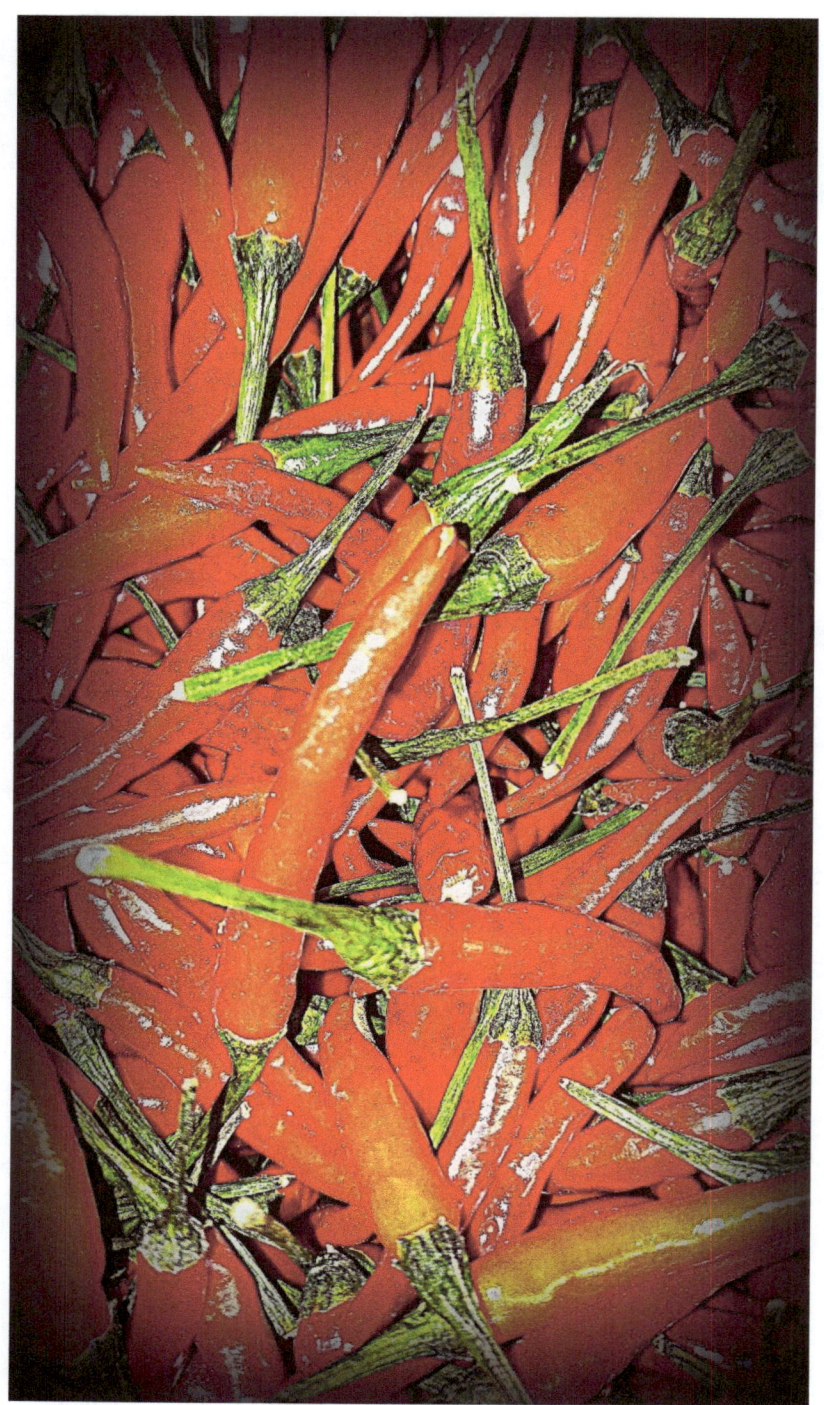

Hot Stuff

# ABOUT THE AUTHOR

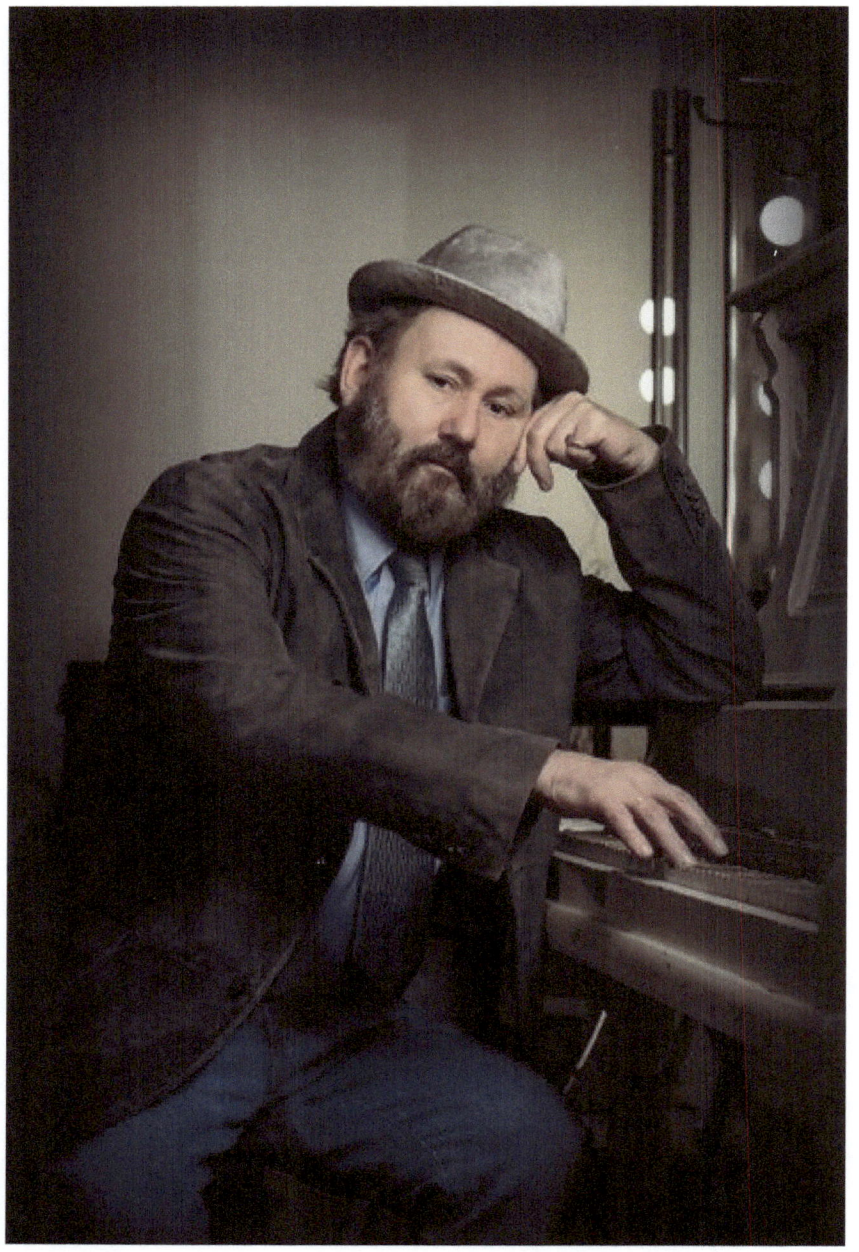

Little is known about the author save he is as mad as
a cut snake and lives in witness protection
somewhere in the green bean casserole belt of Ohio